To Mrs. Lipson,

from Kim   February 2010

D0876431

Capacity to Marry

and the Estate Plan

Kimberly Whaley
Michel Silberfeld
Heather McGee
Helena Likwornik

CANADA LAW BOOK
A Division of the Cartwright Group Ltd.
240 Edward Street, Aurora, Ontario L4G 3S9
www.canadalawbook.ca

© The Cartwright Group Ltd., 2010

Printed in Canada

Library and Archives Canada Cataloguing in Publication

Capacity to marry and the estate plan / Kimberly A. Whaley . . . [et al.].

Includes index.
ISBN 978-0-88804-500-3

1. Marriage law–Canada 2. Capacity and disability–Canada. 3. Marital property–Canada. 4. Older people–Legal status, laws, etc.–Canada
I. Whaley, Kimberly A. (Kimberly Ann), 1965 -

KE544.C36 2010   346.7101'3
C2010-900386-1
KF510.ZA2C36 2010

FOREWORD

It is indeed a pleasure to write the foreword to this timely book. It is timely because the case law on capacity to marry is unclear and the consequences of holding that a person had capacity to marry are significant.

Having previously commented on a couple of Canadian cases that address the issue of capacity to marry (*Banton* and *Barrett*), it is my belief that this book clearly outlines the issues and consequences of a valid marriage. So what is the problem? It is primarily the consequences of a predatory marriage. Such a marriage is easiest to explain by way of an example.

H is an elderly gentleman. W is his, typically much younger, female caregiver. (Usually, the caregiver is a younger female and the other party is an elderly male. But, as the cases illustrate, the roles can also be reversed. Indeed, it is also possible for the two parties to be of the same gender.) H is a widower with grown children. He has a will in which he leaves his estate equally to his children. His health, physical and mental, is failing, and he is lonely and depressed. W becomes his caregiver and sees an opportunity to get her hands on H's assets. She ingratiates herself with H, performing various extra services for him, and he becomes smitten with her. After a period of time, she suggests marriage and he agrees. His family is not informed of the plans and W makes sure that he is isolated from them. The marriage takes place. The officiant and the witnesses are strangers. Then W persuades H to make a new will, in which he leaves her all his estate. He may also appoint W his attorney under a continuing power of attorney for property and a power of attorney for personal care. And he may make improvident gifts to W and transfer funds into joint accounts with himself and W.

The consequences of these events are horrific. If the marriage is valid, H's previous will is revoked by operation of law and his family is disinherited if the will is valid. It is quite possible that the will and powers of attorney are invalid because the tests for capacity to make a will and to grant a power of attorney are quite strict. Moreover, they may be invalid if W exerted undue influence over H. In either case, H will die intestate and W will become entitled to a large portion of the estate under the law of intestate succession. The case of accidental disinheritance leads to a similar result. This happens if H's marriage is valid, so that his prior will is revoked, but he lacks capacity to make a new will. He will then die intestate and again his family is disinherited except to the extent they are entitled to share in the intestacy under Part II of the *Succession Law Reform Act*. W will also have the right under the *Family Law Act* to seek an equalization payment if her net family property is less than his, and the right to claim support from the estate as a dependant under Part V of the *Succession Law Reform Act*.

The problem is that most cases state that the test for capacity to marry is a lenient one. A person has capacity to marry if he understands the nature of the marriage contract and the duties and responsibilities it creates. Further, the contract is said to be a simple one that does not require a high degree of intelligence to comprehend. Under this lenient test, H does not have to understand the property consequences of marriage.

This is, indeed, a serious problem and one that I previously suggested should be revisited by the adoption of a stricter test for the capacity to marry.

By reference to demographic data, the authors make the point that, with an aging population, there will be greater opportunity for predation of older people. In other words, it is likely that we will see more predatory marriages in the future.

The authors discuss the tests for capacity to make a will and powers of attorney, and the capacity to marry in detail and explore the latter by reference to the case law. Further, they emphasize the property consequences of a judicial holding that a marriage is valid and the effect of such a decision on the deceased's family.

Ultimately, they conclude that the test for capacity to marry is defective, because it is too lenient, and make suggestions for changes in the law. I wholeheartedly concur with their conclusions and congratulate them for writing this timely book. I hope that the book will lead to a stricter test for capacity to marry, one that takes into account the property consequences of marriage.

Albert H. Oosterhoff
Professor Emeritus
Faculty of Law
The University of Western Ontario

PREFACE

The notion to write a book on predatory marriages from a legal perspective, and on the capacity to contract marriage, first occurred to me in or about 2006 when in my practice I began to see several cases per year concerning marriages of a predatory nature, with all the usual hallmarks of abuse.

During the course of my interaction with clients, counsel, and our courts, I came to realize the topic begged for closer analysis, insight and increased public awareness.

Dr. Michel Silberfeld, and I were involved in a few such matters where his expertise was sought to assess the issues of consent and capacity to contract marriage.

I approached Michel about collaborating on this book with a view to raising awareness of these important issues given their increasing prevalence. Changing societal norms and challenges including: an aging population; re-marriages; multiple marriages; transient family units; dependancy; vulnerability; and exploitation, to name a few, evidenced that the issues ultimately raised in the book were on the rise and the constraints of the law to effectively adjudicate the issues became therefore obvious.

Ms. Helena Likwornik, my former associate, agreed to collaborate on this project.

We quickly concluded between us that the development of property rights in Canada and the interaction of family law was a crucial and integral part of our analysis. I approached Ms. Heather McGee, a principal of McGee & Fryer, as she then was, prior to her appointment as The Honourable Madam Justice Heather McGee, to seek her involvement. Heather's expertise from a family law perspective was essential to give the analysis context and to identify the deficiencies in the law in its keeping pace with changing societal patterns. Heather was so keen that she actually drafted her initial contribution before the ink on the Canada Law Book contract was dry!

Together, we collaborated on and developed this book with the generous support and assistance of Canada Law Book.

My sincere thanks to my co-authors. On behalf of all of us, I would like to convey our express gratitude to Professor Albert Oosterhoff for his gracious agreement to compose a brilliant Foreword to our book. Special thanks to my estates clerk, Bibi Minoo, who has helped assemble and co-ordinate the contributions, and others who assisted my professional colleagues.

My co-authors have agreed that the authors' royalties generated by this publication will ultimately be used to benefit The Princess Margaret Hospital Foundation.

We trust this book will be a valuable tool in approaching this important and emerging subject matter.

With Thanks,
Kimberly Ann Whaley
January, 2010

AUTHORS' BIOGRAPHICAL NOTES

Kimberly Whaley, C.S., TEP., LLM

Kimberly Whaley is the principal of the law firm, Whaley Estate Litigation. Ms. Whaley practices exclusively in the area of Estate, Trusts, Capacity, Fiduciary, and Power of Attorney Litigation throughout Ontario. She conducts mediations in Estates and Trusts-related matters at estatemediators.ca and is an accredited mediator. She has been designated as a Certified Specialist in Estate and Trusts Law by the Law Society of Upper Canada and continues to be peer rated and listed by the Best Lawyers in Canada in the Specialty of Estates and Trusts. Ms. Whaley is currently the Immediate Past Chair of the OBA Trusts & Estates Executive. She is a member of several committees involved in estates and trusts and contributes regularly to continuing legal education through the CBA, OBA, LSUC STEP (worldwide), the Estate Planning Council of Toronto and in-house organizations. She has been a lecturer, sessional instructor and an Adjunct Lecturer/Professor at Queen's University, Faculty of Law in Appellate Advocacy since 2002 and awarded the Queen's University of Law School Teaching Award. Ms. Whaley is a contributor to the yearly Canada Law Book publication *Key Developments in Estates and Trusts Law in Ontario* and authored the chapter "Passing of Accounts" including "Contested Passings".

Dr. Michel Silberfeld

Dr. Michel Silberfeld has been a specialist in Psychiatry in Ontario from 1976. He worked at The Baycrest Centre for Geriatric Care from 1985 to 2002. Since 1988, until March 2002, he was the founder and co-ordinator of the Competency Clinic. He was involved in the implementation of the Consent and Capacity legislation now current in Ontario. He is a founding Member of the Joint Centre for Bioethics at the University of Toronto. He is the author of more than 60 articles and several book chapters on capacity published in the fields of medicine, law, and bioethics. He co-authored a book with a lawyer, *When the Mind Fails* (University of Toronto Press: 1994). For his work on the Competency Clinic and his work on capacity issues he won one of the Sandoz International Prizes in Gerontology. As a co-principal on a published research project on capacity to give an advance directive, he received along with his co-authors a prize from the American Geriatrics Society. He has been a frequent contributor to legal conferences and to continuing legal education on matters of capacity.

The Honourable Heather A. McGee

Heather McGee is a Judge of the Family Court Branch of the Superior Court of Justice in and for the Province of Ontario. Prior to her appointment she was the founding partner of McGee & Fryer, now Fryer & Associates in Markham, Ontario. She was the President of the Ontario Bar Association in 2005-2006, Chair of the OBA Access to Justice Committee from 2007 to 2009 and served on the Attorney General's Working Group for Family Law from 2004 to 2008. She has also served on various working groups for the OBA with respect to family law, legal aid and access to justice. Madame Justice McGee holds a 1990 Certificate in Mediation and Negotiating from Harvard Law School, and is a past chair of the Newmarket Family Life Centre. In 2004, she obtained her certification in Collaborative Law practice. From 2001 until her appointment to the bench she held an appointment as a Practice Reviewer for the Law Society of Upper Canada. She is the author of numerous articles and papers on family law, estate planning, evidence and justice resourcing.

Helena Likwornik

Helena Likwornik graduated from the University of Toronto law school in 2006 and was called to the Ontario bar in 2007. She is currently legal counsel for the Family Rules Committee and with the Ontario Court of Appeal. Helena Likwornik is working on her PhD at the University of Toronto on the topic of the use of base rates in legal evidence. She is also principal cellist of the Hart House orchestra and a member of the Croydon string quartet.

TABLE OF CONTENTS

TABLE OF CASES

Case Law Available from Canada Law Book

Find case law dating back to 1892 in **BestCase**. This web-based research service contains Canada Law Book's leading law reports and summary services, as well as a comprehensive collection of unreported decisions. Images of reported decisions (as they appear in our law reports) and original judgments are available as PDF files. Contact Canada Law Book's Customer Service at **905-841-6472**, toll free **1-800-263-2037** or **1-800-263-3269**, or online at **www.canadalawbook.ca** for more information.

CHAPTER 1

INTRODUCTION

Marriages between the very old and the very young often make an impression. One evocative term for these relationships is 'May-December' marriages.[1] A more provocative moniker is 'predatory marriages', a term used to emphasize the possible emotional and financial exploitation of the elderly in such an arrangement.

In Canada, the noteworthy cases of *Banton v. Banton*[2] and *Danchuk v. Calderwood*[3] involved marriages between elderly men and much younger women. In both cases, the capacity of the older man to marry, and to make a will, were in issue.

While litigation arising from marriages involving the elderly is still relatively uncommon, we can expect to see more such cases as the number of elderly individuals reaches record highs.

Concern over these marriages arises from the frequent correlation between advanced age and mental decline. The holding in *Banton* that a person can be capable of marriage while incapable for the purposes of making a will is particularly troubling given the financial consequences that accompany marriage.

The *Banton* case will be discussed in greater detail in the chapters that follow. For explanatory purposes, it will suffice to say that Cullity J. held that the test for the capacity to marry is not particularly stringent and requires only that a person understand the nature of the marital relationship and its responsibilities. The holding in *Banton* drew on historical cases such as the 1885 case of *Durham v. Durham*,[4] in which it was stated that a high degree of intelligence is not required to comprehend the significance of entering into a marriage.

---

[1] A.H. Oosterhoff uses the term 'January/December Marriage' for marriages involving especially pronounced age gaps in "Consequences of a January/December Marriage: a Cautionary Tale" (April 1999), 18 E.T.P.J. 261-84.

[2] (1998), 164 D.L.R. (4th) 176, 66 O.T.C. 161 (Gen. Div.), supp. reasons 164 D.L.R. (4th) at p. 244, 83 A.C.W.S. (3d) 531 (Gen. Div.) [hereinafter *Banton*].

[3] (1996), 15 E.T.R. (2d) 193, 67 A.C.W.S. (3d) 418 (B.C.S.C.).

[4] (1885), 10 P.D. 80.

It is troubling that the test for capacity to marry is less stringent than the test for capacity to make a will or to manage one's property, given the significant financial and estate consequences of marriage. Marriage automatically revokes a will. Marriage also brings with it many presumptive entitlements to property and financial support. It is possible, and often desirable in the case of second or third marriages, to avoid or limit these financial consequences by entering into prenuptial or marriage contracts. For elderly individuals with diminished mental capacity, however, these protective measures may not be available. If an elderly individual lacks the requisite capacity to make a new will or to manage his or her own property, but is still found capable of marriage, he or she is denied the opportunity to shield themselves and their family from the financial ramifications of marriage.

As we will see in the chapters that follow, the low threshold traditionally attributed to test the capacity to marry was historically motivated by society's desire to promote marriage. Marriage was valued as an institution for raising children, an instrument of financial security, and a stable building-block of society.

As a result, the law encourages marriage by permitting easy access to legal marriage. While Anglo-American law has in some ways treated marriage as a legal contract governed by the laws applicable to contracts in general, marriage is not subject to the presumptions and principles by which contracts may be voided. In attacking the validity of a marriage, the burden of proof is on those attacking the marriage.

While some historical English case law suggests that the ability to take care of oneself and manage one's own property is a prerequisite for marriage,[5] other authorities, including *Banton*, deny that an inability to manage property is sufficient to establish incapacity to marry.[6] There is currently no legislated standard for capacity that is specific to the decision-making requirements of marriage.

The capacity to marry was first formulated in the context of the first marriages of the young. Marriage was promoted by a permissive threshold, presumably motivated by a perception of marriage as an institution that benefits society by encouraging citizens to marry and raise children. This perspective on marriage is notably romantic, full

---

[5] See for example, *Browning v. Reane* (1812), 161 E.R. 1080, 2 Phill. Ecc. 69; *Spier (Re)*, [1947] W.N. 46 (P.D.): and Halsbury, *Halsbury's Laws of England*, 4th ed. (London: Butterworths, 1974), vol. 22, at para. 911.

[6] See *Whysall v. Whysall*, [1960] P. 52 (P.D.); *Banton, supra*, footnote 2.

of ideals and idealizations. The extent of the ideals and idealizations is revealed, of course, by contrasting them to the pragmatic legal considerations regarding divorce.

Given the context in which the permissive threshold for capacity to marry arose, it is natural to ask whether the same threshold should apply to an aging population, to multiple marriages, and to circumstances involving mental impairment. Mental impairment can present itself in many different forms. Cognitive impairments, including poor judgment, can be revealed by the failure to perform clear tasks of memory. Other impairments are the manifest expression of life-long character traits that often become more exaggerated with age, particularly when coupled with cognitive impairment. In addition, the aged often face such complicating existential circumstances as isolation, illness and impending death.

The forced dependency that comes with illness may also alter the mind. Many who require others to care for them become highly susceptible to undue influence. Because of their state of need, they idealize and fail to criticize. This alone may account for the inclination to favour the latest caregivers, or the providers of terminal care. Memory impairment exaggerates this inclination. Undue influence is not just a function of the perpetrator's force but is also a product of the mentally weakened position of the old and impaired.

The law does recognize certain limited circumstances under which there is an absence of the minimum requisite capacity to marry. For example, the minimum legal age for marriage recognizes that marriage should not be accessible to everyone.[7] But the elderly and the sick, especially those who suffer from some mental impairment, are also vulnerable in marrying. They are vulnerable to lapses in judgment, to failure to adequately take account of past obligations, and to undue influence and coercion. Conflicts related to the wills and estate of the elderly frequently arise from late-life marriages in practice.

Whether something must be done to avoid such conflicts is open to debate. What is indisputable is the tension between the current disparate thresholds for capacity to marry on one hand and testamentary capacity or the capacity to manage one's property on the other. It defies common sense that a person who is not mentally capable of executing a will may nevertheless be mentally capable of

---

[7]   *Marriage Act*, R.S.O. 1990, c. M.3.

marrying and thus effectively revoking his or her existing will and estate plan.

There are at least two potential ways to bridge this gap:

(i)   raise the threshold for capacity to marry; or

(ii) modify the direct link between marriage and property and estate consequences.

Outline of the Chapters to Follow

In the chapters that follow, the authors explore the concept of capacity to marry from the perspective of demographics, historical development, clinical and conceptual frameworks, and trends in the case law.

In Chapter 2, "Demographics", we begin with a discussion on demographics that highlights the expected rise in the number of elderly and emphasizes why any clarity in the law of marriage is needed for the future. Chapter 3, "Marriage and Beyond: Key Concepts", looks at marriage from a variety of perspectives: in the common law; in relation to the law of contract and property; and in existing legislation. In Chapter 4, "Testamentary Freedom", the idea of testamentary freedom is investigated and placed in the context of history and public policy. Chapter 5, "Capacity to Marry", addresses the basic requirements for capacity to marry, the idea of good faith, the possibility of forced marriages, and the possibility of marriage contracts. Chapter 6, "Case Law Review", features a review of both historical and current case law on the topic of capacity to marry. Chapter 7, "Clinical and Conceptual Considerations", addresses a variety of clinical and conceptual considerations about capacity, from clinical assessment criteria to the underlying concept of autonomy. The authors conclude in Chapter 8 that there is currently a tension in the law that should be resolved. Possible solutions to this tension are also raised. It is our hope that this exploration will help lead the way to a resolution of the existing tension in the law, a resolution that will protect the vulnerable and benefit us all.

CHAPTER 2

DEMOGRAPHICS

This chapter discusses demographic trends and highlights the expected rise in the number of elderly. It is against the backdrop of this changing demographic landscape that the need for clarity in the law relating to capacity to marry emerges. Given the predicted steep rise in the number of elderly, there will be more and more circumstances in which those suffering from some degree of mental decline will be entering into the institution of marriage.

The Future: An Aging Population

Today we face what has been aptly called 'a longevity revolution'. At a recent United Nations briefing on aging, Dr. Bernard Starr, Profession of Gerontology at the Marymount Manhattan College stated that "the longevity revolution is indeed a revolution 'comparable to other great revolutions of history, the Renaissance and Industrial Revolution . . . that transformed every aspect of life on this planet:'".[1]

Why are we facing such a revolution? The answer is simple: declining fertility rates and rising life expectancy. Lower fertility rates and medical advances have yielded rises in the absolute number and relative proportion of older people in society. From 1950 to 1998, the median age world-wide increased from 23.5 years to 26.1. It is projected that by 2050, the median age will reach 37.8.[2]

This projected increase in median age will translate into startling increases in the absolute number of older persons worldwide. While there were 580 million older persons in 1998, where 'older person' is defined as a person 60 years of age or older, it is projected that there will be almost two billion older people in 2050.

---

[1] *Towards a Society for All Ages*. International Year of Older Persons, Demographics of Older Persons (United Nations, DPI/1964/G - September 1999).
[2] *Ibid.*

The proportion of the elderly in society is expected to rise to an all-time high in all developed nations. The absolute number of elderly individuals is projected to reach an all-time high. The aging of the population depends on two factors: long lives and a low growth rate. Though long lives and a low growth rate were both rare in the past, both are now becoming the norm around the world. Today more than half of the world's population live in places where fertility is at or below the level needed for long-run intergenerational replacement. Global life expectancy is approaching 70 years. There has been an enormous reduction in mortality, with life expectancy for the two sexes combined now approaching or exceeding 80 in the most developed countries.[3] Current projections indicate that by the year 2050 more than 20% of the population will exceed age 65 in most developed nations. In several, the proportion of those over 65 is expected to reach or exceed 30%. According to the U.N. projections, 21% of the population in the United States will be over the age of 65 by the year 2050.[4] In the United States in 2002, life expectancy was 77.3 years at birth and 18.2 years at age 65. If a person survives to age 65, he or she can expect to live, on average, another 18.2 years.[5]

Life Expectancy in Canada

Life expectancy in Canada has been steadily increasing. According to numbers released by Statistics Canada in January 2008, the average life expectancy has now reached 80.4 years.[6]

The federal agency's numbers are based on data from 2005, with a baby born that year expected to live to 80.4. In 1991, babies were only expected to live to 77.8. In 2004, life expectancy was 80.2.

While women are still expected to live longer than men, the gap between the sexes is shrinking. Girls born in 2005 can expect to live 4.7 years longer than boys, with female life expectancy at 82.7 and male expectancy at 78. In 1991, the gap between the sexes was 6.3 years, with girls expected to live to 80.9 and boys to 74.6.

While Statistics Canada calculated life expectancy, it also studied trends in the deaths reported in 2005. Canadians lived to a mean age of

[3] C. Wilson, "The Century Ahead" (2006), 135 Daedalus, vol. 1, at pp. 5-8.

[4] H.J. Aaron, "Longer Life Spans: Boon or Burden?" (2006), 135 Daedalus, vol. 1, at pp. 9-19.

[5] L.F. Berkman, and M.M. Glymour, "How Society Shapes Aging: The Centrality of Variability" (2006), 135 Daedalus, vol. 1, at pp. 105-114.

[6] CBC News, January 14, 2008, available online at: http://www.cbc.ca/canada/story/2008/01/14/death-stats.html (accessed December 3, 2009).

74.2, compared to 70.9 in 1991. The mean age of women who died was 77.4, while for men it was 71.1. In 1990, 6.6 years was the difference between the two sexes in the average age of death, with women at 74.2.

This data indicates that the Canadian population is aging rapidly. In 2006 there was a 12% increase in persons aged 65 and over since 2001, accounting for more than 4.3 million Canadians. Those aged 85 and over currently represented around 12% of the overall senior population in Canada in 2006. People born between 1946 and 1960 remain the largest population cohort. When this cohort reaches retirement age, the ranks of the elderly can be expected to significantly swell.[7]

Marriage Rates

Although common-law unions have become increasingly common, marriage continues to be the choice for most families. In 2002, 84% of Canadian families were headed by a married couple.[8]

The number of common-law relationships has more than doubled since 1981, when it is estimated that there were approximately 357,000 common-law relationships. This number represented approximately 6% of all couples. By 2001, approximately 14% of all couples were living common-law. Common-law relationships are most prevalent in Quebec, where more than 30% of all families are common-law.

On average, grooms are typically about two-and-a-half years older than their brides. Six percent exchange their first matrimonial vows with someone who has been married before. Eighty-eight percent have raised at least one child.[9]

---

[7] "Census snapshot of Canada-Population [age and sex]" (2006), Statistics Canada, available online at: http://www.statcan.gc.ca/pub/11-008-x/2007006/article/10379-eng.pdf (accessed December 3, 2009).

[8] Statistics Canada Report, CBC News, March 9, 2005, available online at: http://www.cbc.ca/news/background/marriage/ (accessed December 3, 2009).

[9] W. Clark and S. Crompton, "Till death do us part? The risk of first and second marriage dissolution", Statistics Canada article (2006), No. 81, at pp. 23-6.

Marriages by Province and Territory					
	2004	2005	2006	2007[P]	2008[P]
	Number of Marriages				
Canada	**146,242**	**145,842**	**147,084**	**148,296**	**148,831**
Newfoundland and Labrador	2,848	2,793	2,722	2,656	2,650
Prince Edward Island	851	849	844	832	831
Nova Scotia	4,609	4,563	4,513	4,463	4,459
New Brunswick	3,589	3,551	3,497	3,457	3,451
Quebec	21,281	22,244	21,956	22,147	22,050
Ontario	62,425	62,781	63,151	63,718	63,962
Manitoba	5,706	5,714	5,722	5,776	5,804
Saskatchewan	5,050	5,040	5,030	5,095	5,135
Alberta	17,457	17,950	18,632	19,319	19,502
British Columbia	22,076	20,007	20,665	20,479	20,632
Yukon	150	150	152	152	152
Northwest Territories	131	131	129	130	130
Nunavut	69	69	71	72	73

P: preliminary
Source: Statistics Canada, CANSIM, table (for fee) 053-0001. Last modified: 2009-09-29

Age Discrepancies

Where there is a significant discrepancy in the age of two spouses, it is far more frequent for the woman to be much younger than the man. According to the 2001 census, men were 10 or more years older than their spouses in 7% of marriages. The percentage of couples where women were 10 or more years older than their partners was 1%. About 32% of men who are 10 years older than their partners are age 65 or more.[10]

---

[10] M. Boyd and A. Li, "May-December: Canadians in age-discrepant relationships", Statistics Canada article (2003), No. 70, at pp. 29-33.

Research in this area suggests that where there is a significant age difference between spouses, each spouse is likely to diverge from other societal norms as well. For example, people in unions with a considerable age discrepancy are far more likely to be in common-law relationships. They are also more likely to include one partner who is a member of a visible minority group and one who is not. As the age gap increases, the percentage of couples with one Canadian-born and one foreign-born member increases. In relationships with a significant age gap, more often than not, one partner has been previously married while the other has not. In relationships with a significant age gap, the likelihood that one spouse has less than a grade 11 education is greater than for other relationships. Most couples in relationships involving a large age gap have lower combined incomes than do couples who are of a similar age.[11]

Divorce Rates

From 1969 to 1975, the divorce rate rose from 14% of all marriages to 30%. This dramatic increase has been attributed to the passing of the *Divorce Act* in 1968, which extended the grounds for divorce to include so-called "no-fault" divorce based on separation for three years. In 1986, the requisite period of separation was abridged to one year. Well over one-third of Canadian marriages end in divorce before the couple celebrates the 30th anniversary.[12]

In 2003, there were a total of 70,828 legal divorces in Canada. In terms of absolute numbers, the divorce rate peaked in 1987, with 362 divorces for every 100,000 inhabitants. In 2000, there were 231 divorces for every 100,000 inhabitants.[13]

The highest recorded divorce rate was 26.2 per 1,000 couples after three years of marriage. The likelihood of divorce declined slightly with each subsequent year of marriage. Twenty-three percent of first marriages end in dissolution after 11 years of matrimony. Nine percent of first marriages end in the death of a spouse after 34 years together.[14]

---

[11] *Ibid.*, at pp. 29-33.
[12] Clark and Crompton, *ibid.*, footnote 9, at pp. 23-6.
[13] Statistics Canada Report, *ibid.,* footnote 8.
[14] Clark and Crompton, *ibid.*, footnote 9, at pp. 23-6.

Divorces by Province and Territory					
	2001	2002	2003	2004	2005
	Number of Divorces				
Canada	**71,110**	**70,155**	**70,828**	**69,644**	**71,269**
Newfoundland and Labrador	755	842	662	837	789
Prince Edward Island	246	258	281	293	283
Nova Scotia	1,945	1,990	1,907	2,000	1,961
New Brunswick	1,570	1,461	1,450	1,415	1,444
Quebec	17,094	16,499	16,738	15,999	15,423
Ontario	26,516	26,170	27,513	26,374	28,805
Manitoba	2,480	2,396	2,352	2,333	2,429
Saskatchewan	1,955	1,959	1,992	1,875	1,922
Alberta	8,252	8,291	7,960	8,317	8,075
British Columbia	10,115	10,125	9,820	10,049	9,954
Yukon Territory	91	90	87	66	109
Northwest Territories	83	68	62	71	65
Nunavut	8	6	4	15	10
Source: Statistics Canada, CANSIM, tables (for fee) 53-0002 and 101-6501. Last modified: 2009-09-28					

Remarriage

When asked the question, "Do you think you will ever marry again?" less than a quarter of divorced Canadians answered "Yes". Between 1990 and 2006, the proportion of divorced people stating that they intended to remarry decreased from 26% to 22%. In contrast, more than six out of 10 divorced Canadians stated that they do not wish to remarry. In 1990, it was roughly five out of 10 divorced Canadians.[15]

---

[15] P. Beaupré, "I do . . . Take two? Changes in intentions to remarry among divorced Canadians during the past 20 years", Statistics Canada, Analytical Studies, July 17, 2007, available online at: www.statcan.gc.ca (accessed December 3, 2009).

Statistics Canada numbers from 2003 indicated that the number of Canadians getting divorced more than once is on the rise. For couples where a husband had been divorced at least once, the number of marriage dissolutions had tripled in three decades.

In 2003, 16.2 % of husbands filing for divorce had at least one divorce behind them. By comparison, the rate in 1973 was only 5.2 %. The numbers were similar for wives. In 1973, only 5.4% of women getting divorced had been previously divorced; by 2003, that number had risen to 15.7%.[16]

Forty-three percent of Canadian adults whose first marriage ends in divorce marry again. Where marriage ends in the death of a first spouse, only 16% remarry. One in five Canadians who remarry find their second spouse within an average of 7.6 years. Less than 1% of people over 25 marry more than twice. Of this group, on average, the individual enters his or her third marriage at the age of 46 and marries someone who has also been married before.[17]

People who enter into multiple marriages tend to demonstrate certain characteristic personality and behaviour traits. Both men and women who marry multiple times tend to have a higher level of anxiety than those who marry only once or twice. Those who enter into serial marriages are less likely than those who marry only once to cite marriage as important to their happiness.[18]

Consequences of Demographic Trends

As the average age of the population increases, there will likely be a rise in the number of the frail and the disabled. Physical and mental capacities decline with age. In addition to deteriorating health, sensory systems and bodily strength, one of the first things to decline markedly in old age is the capacity to learn. Almost five times as many people over 85 as those under 85 suffer from chronic impairments and exhibit low functional scores across a wide range of physical, cognitive, and social indicators. Indicators of well-being such as life satisfaction, social integration and a positive attitude towards life tend to decline for those over 65.[19]

---

[16] Statistics Canada Report, *ibid.,* footnote 8.

[17] Clark and Crompton, *ibid.,* footnote 9, at pp. 23-6.

[18] *Ibid.,* at pp. 23-6.

[19] S. Harper, "Mature Societies: Planning For Our Future Selves" (2006), 135 Daedalus, vol. 1, at pp. 20-31.

There are also many brain diseases that express themselves as a progressive loss of intellectual function. Vascular, metabolic, infectious, neoplastic, traumatic, and degenerative disorders can all present with symptoms of dementia. In the United States, multi-infarct dementia has long been considered the second most common basis for late-life dementia. Parkinson's disease associated dementia and Lewy body dementia are also common in the elderly.[20]

Dementia, especially Alzheimer's disease, leads to a gradual deterioration in many basic human characteristics including intentionality, independence, identity and social integration. According to the Berlin study of aging, 5% of 70 year olds suffer from some form of dementia including Alzheimer's. This percentage increases to 10 - 15% for 80 year olds and to 50% for those 90 to 100 years of age. Age is the most important risk factor for Alzheimer's disease. The rates of illness increase steadily with age.[21]

The expansion of the elderly population is likely to see a rise in the number of spouses who outlive their partners, thereby increasing the likelihood of additional marriages.[22]

In the cases discussed in the chapters that follow, large age discrepancies are the norm. Often, one member of the couple is frail and sometimes cognitively impaired. We will also often see a recurring thread of large discrepancy in net financial worth.

The law relating to capacity to marry is unclear. Marriage carries significant consequences for an individual's finances and estate. Greater clarity in this area is required, with growing numbers of elderly individuals who may be experiencing some mental decline entering into marriage.

---

[20] D.J. Selkoe, "The Aging Mind: Deciphering Alzheimer's Disease and its Antecedents" (2006), 135 Daedalus, vol. 1, at pp. 58-67; J.L. Cummings and Z.S. Khachaturian, *Definitions and diagnostic criteria, in clinical diagnosis and management of Alzheimer's disease*, S. Gauthier, ed. (London: Martin Dunitz Ltd., 1999), at pp. 3-13.

[21] J.L. Cummings and Z.S. Khachaturian, *ibid.*, at pp. 3-13.

[22] "Census snapshot of Canada-population [age and sex]", *ibid.*, footnote 7.

CHAPTER 3

MARRIAGE AND BEYOND: KEY CONCEPTS

This chapter looks at the institution of marriage from a variety of perspectives: in the common law, in relation to the law of contract and property, and in existing legislation. In order to make sense of the existing standard for capacity to marry and to put into perspective any discussion of how this standard may be reformed, it is important to understand what marriage means to us as a society. The development of the law relating to marriage is a good place to start.

Marriage and the Common Law

(1) Introduction

Modern family law is self-consciously designed around furthering gender equality. Among the recurrent themes that play throughout the law around the definition of family are uniformity versus diversity, form versus function, and the normative versus the empirical.

Society has rapidly transformed in relation to the construct of marriage. There has been an overall decline in marriage, and over half of common-law relationships now involve children. There are also more single-parent families, there has been a decline in fertility rates, and 70% of women with children are now part of the paid labour force. In addition, 37% of marriages are expected to end within 30 years.

There is also a unique tension in family law between the public and private, with significant philosophical divides in terms of the role that the state should play in the married lives of its members. While the law imposes strict and substantial rights and obligations attaching to marriage, the justification for most of these impositions is based on a marital model that involves children. It is quite questionable whether the law should impose in the same way on childless unions.

(2)   Definition of Marriage

A number of judicial decisions between 2003 and 2005 redefined the definition of marriage. They held that that the traditional common law definition of "marriage" as "the voluntary union for life of one man and one woman to the exclusion of all others" contravened s. 15 of the *Canadian Charter of Rights and Freedoms*,[1] by precluding same-sex marriage such that the definition could not be saved by s. 1 of the Charter. The current definition is therefore "the voluntary or lawful union of two persons to the exclusion of all others".[2]

(3)   Judicial Dicta on Marriage

Justice Gonthier, speaking for himself and Lamer C.J.C., La Forest and Major J.J. (concurring, dissenting) made the following statement about marriage:

> The decision to marry includes the acceptance of various legal consequences incident to the institution of marriage, including the obligation of mutual support between spouses and the support and raising of children of the marriage. In my view, freedom of choice and the contractual nature of marriage are crucial to understanding why distinctions premised on marital status are not necessarily discriminatory: Where individuals choose not to marry, it would undermine the choice they have made if the state were to impose upon them the very same burdens and benefits which it imposes upon married persons.[3]

In *Miron*, Gonthier J. referred to the remarks made by Michael D.A. Freeman and Christina M. Lyon on marriage:

> "... marriage is a voluntary institution in which the parties express their willingness to commit themselves to each other for life. Whether they are completely cognisant of all the legal effects of such a commitment is immaterial; the commitment is made, nevertheless, and marital rights and obligations inevitably follow. Cohabiting couples do not make that same commitment, and rights and duties akin to marriage should not as a result follow. The danger with imposing the incidents of marriage on a cohabiting couple is that it constitutes a denial of a fundamental freedom."[4]

---

[1]   Part I of the *Constitution Act, 1982*, being Schedule B to the *Canada Act 1982* (U.K.), 1982, c. 11.

[2]   J.D. Payne and M.A. Payne, *Canadian Family Law*, 3rd ed. (Toronto: Irwin Law, 2008), at p. 24.

[3]   *Miron v. Trudel* (1995), 124 D.L.R. (4th) 693, [1995] S.C.R. 418, at para. 46.

In *Halpern v. Canada (Attorney General)*,[5] a case in which the Ontario Court of Appeal declared the existing common law definition of marriage invalid to the extent that it refers to "one man and one woman" and reformulated the common law definition as "the voluntary union for life of two persons to the exclusion of all others", the court made the following comments about marriage and the capacity to enter into it:

> The common law rule of marriage is not itself a complex law — indeed it is straightforward and simple. In the final analysis it does no more than define who may participate in the societal institution of marriage. Thus, this common law rule by definition is itself only a definition. That is, it defines who has the capacity to marry.[6]

Later, the court elaborates further that:

> Marriage is, without dispute, one of the most significant forms of personal relationships. For centuries, marriage has been a basic element of social organization in societies around the world. Through the institution of marriage, individuals can publicly express their love and commitment to each other. Through this institution, society publicly recognizes expressions of love and commitment between individuals, granting them respect and legitimacy as a couple. This public recognition and sanction of marital relationships reflect society's approbation of the personal hopes, desires and aspirations that underlie loving, committed conjugal relationships. This can only enhance an individual's sense of self-worth and dignity.[7]

(4)   History and Development of Marriage and Property

Family law in Ontario has its origins in the common law of England. At common law, there was a unity of legal personality between husband and wife. When a man and woman married, legally the wife had no standing in her own right and any property that she owned became that of her husband. The wife could not keep her own earnings if she worked outside the home. The wife could not enter into contracts. Custody of the children went to the husband.

---

[4]   M.D.A. Freeman and C.M. Lyon, *Cohabitation without Marriage* (Aldershot, Hants.: Gower, 1983), at p. 191, quoted in *Miron v. Trudel, supra*, at para. 46.

[5]   (2002), 215 D.L.R. (4th) 223, 60 O.R. (3d) 321 (S.C.J. (Div. Ct.)), affd 225 D.L.R. (4th) 529, 65 O.R. (3d) 161 (C.A.), motion to quash granted [2003] S.C.C.A. No. 337 (QL) [hereinafter *Halpern*].

[6]   *Supra*, at para. 294 (S.C.J.).

[7]   *Halpern, supra*, footnote 5, at para. 5 (C.A.).

The only protection a wife had for property that she brought into the marriage was that her husband could not alienate the land without her approval. The law of dower also allowed that at the husband's death any land owned by the wife prior to marriage reverted to her. At the husband's death, the wife received a one-third inchoate life interest in all lands held by the husband.

The husband did have an obligation to support his family while the wife had no such responsibility, provided that the husband and wife were living together. For example, if they were living together the wife could use the husband's credit to buy the 'necessaries' of life. However, the husband could give notice that the wife was not allowed to use his credit if he desired. If the wife left the husband he did not have to support her in any manner.

Throughout the 1800s and early 1900s there was much sympathy for abused and abandoned wives in the Court of Chancery. Many acknowledged the need for reform to better protect wives, especially regarding property brought into the marriage by the wife. However, the ideas for reform were not based on giving wives equality but instead on protecting them from unscrupulous husbands. Modest reforms allowed wives to have separate property but only when done through a trust, giving a third party trustee control over the property.[8] While this kept the husband from controlling the wife's property, it also kept the property out of the hands of the wife.

The first property Act in Upper Canada was the *Married Women's Property Act* of 1859.[9] This Act allowed property inherited by the wife to remain as a separate estate but still left the property under the control of a trustee, usually the husband.[10] The Act also provided wives with the ability to retain their own earnings but only if they received a protection order because of an irresponsible, abusive, or absent husband.[11]

Further reforms in 1872 and 1873 allowed all married women to retain their own earnings and the ability to hold and dispose of personal property, but not real property. Married women were finally allowed to acquire, hold and dispose of real property with the passage of the *Married Women's Property Act, 1884.*[12]

---

[8]   L. Chambers, *Married Women and Property Law in Victorian Ontario* (Toronto: University of Toronto Press, 1997), at p. 54.

[9]   Consolidated Statutes of Upper Canada, 1859, c. 73.

[10]   *Ibid.*, at p. 71.

[11]   *Ibid.*

[12]   S.O. 1884, c. 19.

Additionally, married women were for the first time granted the right to sue and be sued on their own behalf, but not against a spouse. The *Married Women's Property Act, 1984,* left undisturbed provisions that women could not acquire any interest in property obtained during the marriage, and that they had no legal responsibility for the maintenance of the family.

These laws with respect to marriage remained in place for nearly 100 years in Ontario despite concurrent progressions in the treatment and recognition of women as spouses in common-law relationships. It was not until the passage of the *Family Law Reform Act*[13] (*"FLRA"*) in 1978 that new reforms were introduced into family law. In a historical context, these reforms were quite startling.

Leading up to the passage of the *FLRA*, the Ontario Law Reform Commission conducted a Family Law Study which resulted in the release of The Report on Family Law in 1974 ("the Report"). The Report recommended two different regimes for division of assets on marriage breakdown, with one regime based on a partnership model for families with the traditional wage-earner and homemaker, and the other on a separate property model for spouses who were both fully employed outside the home. The Report promoted the concept of spouses being able to choose which model to adopt. The Report also created the process of equalizing the value of the combined assets acquired during the marriage.

The *FLRA* did not follow all the recommendations contained in the Report. One significant change in the Act was that it abolished the unity of legal personality between husband and wife, allowing spouses to sue each other for the first time. This ability gave rise to our modern concept of family law as a set of entitlements vis-à-vis spouses irrespective of blameworthy conduct.

Property reform was based on a departure from the traditional view of marriage. The *FLRA* incorporated only the separate property model from the recommendations in the 1974 Report. Marriage was now an economic partnership between husband and wife, who each retained their personal and legal autonomy. In other words, an individual's ownership of assets and responsibility for debts remained undisturbed by the act of marriage. Indeed, it remains a common misperception to this day that a spouse is liable for another spouse's debts, or has ownership in a spouse's assets. Neither has any

---

[13]   S.O. 1978, c. 2.

operation, but for deliberate arrangements in which a spouse co-signs or guarantees a mortgage, or title is placed into joint ownership.

Within the new framework of the *FLRA*, both husband and wife were to benefit or suffer disadvantage in an equal manner, so that upon separation were one spouse in a more advantageous position as a result of the ownership of assets, absence of debt, or greater income, the other spouse held certain claims that could be advanced.

Such claims were not to be decided solely based on ownership of assets, but on the use of specific assets. Assets were divided into family and non-family assets based on the use of the asset and divided accordingly.

The current governing legislation in Ontario, the *Family Law Act*[14] ("*FLA*"), came into force within a relatively short period, being proclaimed in 1986. The guiding principal of marriage as an economic partnership was firmly cemented into the *FLA*. The distinction between family and non-family assets was removed, ending eight years of uneven judicial findings. Any assets held on the date of separation by either party were family assets, but for assets which were excluded by operation of law or a domestic contract.

(5) Formal and Essential Validity

Marriage law is divided between the federal and provincial governments in Canada. The federal government, through s. 91(26) of the *Constitution Act, 1867*, regulates marriage and divorce. The provincial government, through s. 92(12), regulates the solemnization of marriage. Essential validity, under federal jurisdiction, concerns the legal capacity of parties to marry, in other words, who can marry. Formal validity, under provincial jurisdiction, concerns the ceremonial and evidentiary requirements that must be met before a marriage is valid.

Provincial legislation sets out the steps one must take in order to have a valid marriage in the province. The Ontario *Marriage Act*[15] ("*Marriage Act*") lays out these requirements. By legislating age and consent requirements for obtaining a marriage licence, the province has stepped into what is arguably federal territory of who can marry. One must be 18 years old or have the written consent of both parents to obtain a marriage licence.[16] The Act also prohibits granting a

---

[14] R.S.O. 1990, c. F.3.
[15] R.S.O. 1990, c. M.3.
[16] *Ibid.*, s. 5.

licence or solemnizing the marriage of any person who "lacks mental capacity to marry by reason of being under the influence of intoxicating liquor or drugs or for any other reason".[17]

Very little federal legislation exists for the requirements of essential validity for marriage. The *Marriage (Prohibited Degrees) Act*,[18] sets out the prohibition against marrying someone related by consanguinity, affinity, or adoption. Section 2 of the *Civil Marriage Act*,[19] defines marriage as "the lawful union of two persons to the exclusion of all others", thereby opening marriage to same-sex couples. Other than these two Acts, one must rely on the English and Canadian common law to find other aspects relating to the requirements for essential validity to marry.

Other requirements for a valid marriage, arising from the common law, are the ability to consummate the marriage, that no prior marriage continues to be valid, and adequate consent. Consent has several requirements of its own; it must be freely given with the requisite understanding, and not under mistake or duress.

It is the law of the place where the marriage was contracted (*lex loci celebrationis*) that defines formal validity. The burden rests upon anyone questioning the validity of marriage to show that the requirements of the location of the marriage celebration were not met. In Canada, marriage formalities are part of the provincial government's domain. In Ontario, for example, the *Marriage Act* regulates and governs the solemnization of marriage. This legislation stipulates that a valid marriage must be under the authority of a licence issued in accordance with this Act or the publication of banns. It specifies those with the authority to marry and provides that any person who is of the age of majority may obtain a licence or be married under the authority of the publication of banns, provided no lawful cause exists to hinder the solemnization.

Despite the requirements for formal validity, s. 31 of the *Marriage Act* provides that:

> [i]f the parties to a marriage solemnized in good faith and intended to be in compliance with this Act are not under a legal disqualification to contract such marriage and after such solemnization have lived together and cohabited as a married couple, such marriage shall be deemed a valid marriage, although the person who solemnized the marriage was not

---

[17] *Ibid.*, s. 7.
[18] S.C. 1990, c. 46.
[19] S.C. 2005, c. 33.

authorized to solemnize marriage, and despite the absence of or any irregularity or insufficiency in the publication of banns or the issue of the licence.

What a valid marriage does require is the voluntary consent of both parties and the absence of any legal incapacity to marry.[20] Of particular interest is the provision on "persons lacking mental capacity" in the *Marriage Act*:

> 7. No person shall issue a licence to or solemnize the marriage of any person who, based on what he or she knows or has reasonable grounds to believe, lacks mental capacity to marry by reason of being under the influence of intoxicating liquor or drugs or for any other reason.

More will be said in Chapter 5, "Capacity to Marry".

(6) Void and Voidable

A void marriage is one that is null and void from the start (*void ab initio*). In law, it is regarded as though it never happened. A voidable marriage, on the other hand, is treated in law as valid unless and until it is annulled by a court of competent jurisdiction.

In principle, the absence of consent, irrespective of its kind, should render a marriage void. Judicial decisions, have, however, differed on their interpretation of a marriage as void or voidable depending on the applicable type of absence of consent.[21]

(a) Unsoundness of Mind: Alcohol and Drug Intoxication

Excessive drug or alcohol consumption may negate freedom to consent to marry. The test is whether the person was incapable of understanding the ceremony of marriage and the duties and responsibilities that flow from marriage. The burden of proof lies with the person who seeks to challenge the marriage.[22]

(b) Duress

A marriage is voidable where there was improper pressure placed on a person thereby undermining his or her ability to consent of his or her own volition. Fear is usually an implicit element of duress,

---

[20] *Moss v. Moss*, [1897] P. 263, at p. 268.

[21] J.D. Payne and M.A. Payne, *Canadian Family Law*, 3rd. ed. (Toronto: Irwin Law, 2008), at pp. 31-32.

[22] *Ibid.*, at p. 32.

although no physical force need be exerted. Some cases have found a marriage voidable, at the option only of the party under duress, while others have found it *void ab initio.*[23]

(c)   Fraud

Inducing a person to marry with fraudulent misrepresentations will not remove consent so long as there is no mistake as to the identity of the person one is marrying:

> No degree of deception can avail to set aside a contract of marriage duly celebrated by consenting parties with the capacity to enter into the marriage.[24]

In another case, it was held that:

> No marriage shall be held void merely upon proof that it had been contracted upon false representations, and that but for such contrivances, consent never would have been obtained. Unless the party imposed upon has been deceived as to the person, and thus has given no consent at all, there is no degree of deception which can avail to set aside a contract of marriage knowingly made.[25]

One can easily imagine that otherwise a large number of marriages would be voidable upon this basis.

(d)   Mistake

Only mistake as to the identity of the person or mistake as to the nature of the ceremony can render a marriage void for lack of consent. Mistake as to the attributes of the person one married, for example, respecting age, health, virginity or wealth, do not negate consent to marry. In one case, a woman's wilful concealment of her pregnancy by another man at the time of the marriage was held not to make the marriage void or voidable on the basis of the husband's absence of consent.[26] However, where there is mistake as to the nature of the ceremony, that is, where a marriage ceremony is believed to be a celebration of another nature, consent may be vitiated.

---

[23]   *Ibid.*, at p. 33.
[24]   *Kokkalas v. Kokkalas* (1965), 50 D.L.R. (2d) 193 at p. 194, 51 W.W.R. 511 (Sask. Q.B.).
[25]   *Swift v. Kelly* (1835), 12 E.R. 648 (H.L.), at p. 661.
[26]   *Ibid*, footnote 21, at p. 34; *Ford v. Stier*, [1896] P. 1.

(e)   Intention and Motive

While intent to marry is a necessary element for a valid marriage, motive is irrelevant:

> In English law, while the purely sham marriage is of no effect, e.g., a masquerade, theatre performance, party entertainment, things of that kind, generally the mental reservations or motive of the parties, or one of them, will not serve to destroy the validity of the ceremony.

> So, the parties were held to their mutual promises in *Brooks-Bischoffberger v. Brooks-Bischoffberger* (1930), 149 A. 606 at 607, 129 Me. 52, where a marriage performed through the dare of a third party was held to be valid, Dunn J. observing that "marriage is a status wherein public policy rises superior to mere sympathy"; or to win a bet, *Parker v. Parker* (1757), 2 Lee, 382, 161 E.R. 377; to obtain employment open only to married persons, *Crouch v. Wartenberg* (1920), 104 S.E. 117, 11 A.L.R. 212, 91 W. Va. 91 (West Virginia C.A.); to comply with the terms of a settlement conferring gifts subject to the beneficiary's marriage, *Coppo v. Coppo* (1937), 297 N.Y.S. 744, 163 Misc. 249; to avoid a court martial, *Dumoulin v. Druitt* (1860), 13 Ir. C.L. 212 (Q.B.).

> In all those cases the protests of the petitioner that the marriage was no more than a sham, an event which one or both of the parties regarded as fictitious or simulated, went unheard, English law considering it irrelevant to consider the motives which prompt a party to enter into the union.[27]

A marriage is also not invalidated simply because it was entered into in order to evade immigration regulations.

Marriage and Contract Law

In multiple ways, marriage is much more than a contract. It is also a status that is conferred on individuals by the state. Given the public character of marriage, there are general laws that dictate and control the rights, obligations, and incidents of marriage, quite apart from the intentions or desires of the particular parties to the marriage. The principle of contractual autonomy does, however, have an application in the marital context.[28]

---

[27] *Fernandez v. Fernandez* (1983), 21 Man. R. (2d) 254, 34 R.F.L. (2d) 249 at pp. 253-54 (Q.B.), Wilson J., as cited in J.D. Payne and M.A. Payne, *ibid.*, footnote 21, at pp. 35-36.

[28] Payne and Payne, *ibid.*, at p. 23.

A contract is an agreement that gives rise to enforceable obligations that are enforced or recognized by law. Contractual obligations are distinguishable from other legal obligations on the basis that they arise from agreement between contracting parties.[29]

A contract is said to be valid where the following elements are present: offer, acceptance and consideration. The doctrine of consideration is based upon the idea of reciprocity: "something of value in the eye of the law".[30]

An offer is an expression of willingness to contract on specified terms where there is the intention for the agreement to become binding upon acceptance.[31] An acceptance is a final expression of assent to the terms of an offer.[32]

The requirement of consideration to form a binding contract may be viewed as an obstacle to conceiving of marriage as a contract. "[N]atural affection of itself is not a sufficient consideration".[33] For example, in *Thomas v. Thomas*,[34] the wish of a testator that his widow live in his house was not part of the consideration for the executors' promise that she might do so. Similarly, in *White v. Bluett*,[35] it was held that since a son had "no right" to bore his father with complaints, his promise not to do so, in exchange for his father's promise not to sue him on a promissory note, did not constitute consideration.

Among the circumstances that qualify as terminating an offer is what is called 'supervening incapacity'. If an offeror becomes mentally incapable he or she is not bound by an acceptance made after the incapacity became known to the offeree, or after the offeror's property became subject to the protection of the state.[36]

The intention to contract is a necessary ingredient for a binding contract. It is for this reason that most domestic arrangements have been found to lack contractual force. For example, in *Balfour v. Balfour*,[37] where a husband had promised to pay his wife a certain sum

---

29 G.H. Treitel, *The Law of Contract*, 11th ed. (London: Sweet & Maxwell, 2003), Introduction.

30 *Thomas v. Thomas* (1842), 2 Q.B. 851, at p. 859.

31 Treitel, *ibid.*, footnote 29, at p. 8.

32 Treitel, *ibid.*, footnote 29, at p. 16.

33 *Bret v. JS* (1600), 78 E.R. 987, Cro. Eliz. 756; *Mansukhani v. Sharkey* (1992), 24 H.L.R. 600, [1992] 2 E.G.L.R. 105.

34 *Supra*, footnote 30.

35 (1853), 23 L.J. Ex. 36.

36 Treitel, *ibid.*, footnote 29, at p. 45.

37 [1919] 2 K.B. 571 (C.A.).

by way of an allowance, the wife's attempt to enforce this promise as legally binding failed. Lord Atkin held that the wife had not provided consideration and also that the parties did not intend the arrangement to be legally binding.

At common law, someone who suffers a loss as a result of relying on a fraudulent statement can recover damages. The following conditions are sufficient for a statement to qualify as fraudulent:

(i)   it is made with the knowledge of its falsity;

(ii) it is made without a belief in its truth; or

(iii) it is made with reckless disregard to whether it is true or false.[38]

Where consent to a contract has been obtained by some form of pressure that the law regards improper, the pressured party may be entitled to relief under the common law of duress and/or the equitable rules of undue influence.[39]

While the old strict requirement of a threat of violence is no longer required to attract the common law doctrine of duress, the equitable principle of pressure or 'undue influence' is still broader.[40]

To give rise to the presumption of undue influence, it must be established that there existed a relationship between A and B by virtue of which B either in fact reposed trust and confidence in A or is taken as a matter of law to have done so. Such relationships include those where the relationship between the two parties is that of parent and child, guardian and ward, religious advisor and disciple, doctor and patient, solicitor and client, and trustee and *cestui que* trust. The presumption has been held to apply to a transaction between fiancés, where the woman agreed, in return for a small immediate payment, to give up large sums which were to accrue to her as a widow.[41] In another case, the gift of an extravagant engagement ring did not attract a similar presumption.[42]

Some case law supports the idea that a marked disparity in bargaining power may give rise to an entitlement to relief if one party has taken unfair advantage of this situation.[43]

---

[38] Treitel, *ibid.*, footnote 29, at p. 343.

[39] *Ibid.*, at p. 405.

[40] *Ibid.*, at p. 409.

[41] *Lloyds Bank Ltd. (Re)*, [1931] 1 Ch. 289.

[42] *Zamet v. Hyman*, [1961] 1 W.L.R. 1442, [1961] 3 All E.R. 933 (C.A.).

[43] G.H. Treitel, *The Law of Contract*, 11th ed. (London: Sweet & Maxwell, 2003), at p. 421.

A person can also recover money or property transferred under circumstances of oppression. A contract is considered 'illegal' if one party was forced by another to enter into it. In *Atkinson v. Denby*,[44] for example, an insolvent debtor offered to pay his creditors a dividend of 5 shillings on the pound. All the creditors were willing to accept the dividend in full settlement of their claims, except the defendant, who said he would accept it only if the debtor first paid him £50. The debtor did so, but was later allowed to recover the £50 on the ground that he had been forced to agree to defraud the other creditors. Oppression permitting recovery may arise not just from the conduct of the other party, but also from extraneous circumstances.

The concepts of fraud and undue influence all have some potential application to marriage when viewed in contractual terms. The review of case law below will further illuminate this aspect of our subject.

Marriage and Property Law

(1)   Introduction of Basic Property Concepts

Given the intimate relationship between property rights and the institution of marriage, any discussion about the law as it relates to marriage would be incomplete without at least a brief introduction to some basic principles of property law.

Blackstone defined property as the "sole and despotic dominion which one man claims and exercises over the external things of the world, in total exclusion of the right of any other individual in the universe".[45] Similarly John Locke, an early British philosopher, conceived of the right of property as an inalienable natural right of the individual, free from interference by others and by the state.[46] Jeremy Bentham took the contrasting view that property is not a natural right but rather a creature of law.[47]

The concepts of 'ownership', 'title' and 'possession' are all central to any thorough understanding of property. In the context of

---

[44]   (1862), 158 E.R. 749, 7 H. & N. 934.

[45]   2Bl. Comm., at pp. 2-3.

[46]   W.G. Friedmann, *Law in a Changing Society*, 2nd ed. (New York: Columbia University Press, 1972), at p. 93.

[47]   J. Bentham, "Principles of the Civil Code", in E. Dupont, ed.; R. Hildreth, trans., *Theory of Legislation*, vol. 1 (Boston: Weeks, Jordan & Co., 1840), at p. 112.

land, a person does not own land, but rather owns the fee simple estate or some other interest in the land. It is the Crown that has allodial ownership. Ownership comes with a multitude of rights, powers, privileges and immunities. Ownership of land comes with the right to use it, live on it, farm it, recover minerals from it, sell it, mortgage it, lease it, grant a right of way over it, protect it from trespass and nuisance, and dispose of it by will or pass it on an intestacy.[48]

The term 'title' can usually be used interchangeably with 'ownership' although there a few circumstances in which this is not the case. For example, there is a legal distinction between legal title to property and beneficial ownership.[49]

'Possession' may be 'actual' or 'constructive'. That is, it can be in 'deed' or in 'law'. In law a person has constructive possession of all land to which he or she has registered title except to the extent that someone else occupies it adversely.[50]

(2) Promissory Estoppel

Promissory estoppel is another legal concept that is relevant to the backdrop of our discussion. Where a promise is made by one party to a contract to another, that the contract will be waived or not enforced, in whole or in part, and this promise is acted upon, promissory estoppel may be engaged and may prevent the promisor from taking action to enforce the contract against the promise.[51]

While in law, a contract requires consideration, a promise not to follow through on a contract, or that the contract will be waived or not enforced in whole or in part, has no consideration and would therefore, on the strict application of common law principles, be unenforceable.

However, equity will step in to address an injustice that the common law overlooks. Therefore, equity stepped in with a new variation of estoppel and held that when a person promises not to follow through on a contract, even though there may be no consideration to that specific promise, and therefore no contract at law in this regard, the promisor is estopped from enforcing the

---

[48] A. Warner La Forest, *Anger & Honsberger Law of Real Property*, 3rd ed., looseleaf (Toronto: Canada Law Book, October, 2008), Part I.

[49] *Ibid.*

[50] *Ibid.*, at p. 1-5.

[51] Online at: http://www.duhaime.org/LegalDictionary.aspx (accessed December 3, 2009).

contract for which he or she had extended his or her promise not to enforce.

In this way, promissory estoppel can be understood as an extension of the general principle of equity that requires every party to come to the court with 'clean hands'. The 'clean hands' doctrine is an equitable defence in which the defendant argues that the plaintiff is not entitled to obtain an equitable remedy on account of the fact that the plaintiff has acted in bad faith with respect to the subject of the complaint, *i.e.*, with 'unclean hands'. The defendant has the burden of proof to show that the plaintiff is not acting in good faith. The doctrine is often stated as "those seeking equity must do equity" or "equity must come with clean hands". A defendant's unclean hands can also be claimed and proven by the plaintiff to claim other equitable remedies and to prevent that defendant from asserting equitable affirmative defences. In other words, 'unclean hands' can be used offensively by the plaintiff as well as defensively by the defendant.

In *Maracle v. Travellers Co. of Canada*[52] it was stated that:

> The principles of promissory estoppel are well settled. The party relying on the doctrine must establish that the other party has, by words or conduct, made a promise or assurance which was intended to affect their legal relationship and to be acted on. Furthermore, the representee must establish that, in reliance on the representation, he acted on it or in some way changed his position.

(3) Marital Property

The late 1970s and early 1980s saw extensive legislative reform respecting matrimonial property. This was in response to the recognition that the common law and equitable regime of separate property often resulted in an unfair distribution of the assets acquired through spouses' joint efforts when their relationship ended. Accordingly, legislation currently exists in every province mandating the sharing of certain marital property. Family law in Canada generally imposes support obligation on life partners, regardless of whether they are married.

Historically, at common law, upon marriage, the wife lost almost all her right to the benefits of property ownership. The husband acquired ownership of the wife's personal property with the exception

---

[52] (1991), 80 D.L.R. (4th) 652, [1991] 2 S.C.R. 50, at para. 13.

of personal items and the right to the profits of her real property. Even a married woman's wages belonged to her husband.[53]

The Doctrine of Legal Unity prescribed that in law, a husband and wife were one person and that person was the husband. Married women lost the right to contract, to sue in tort and to dispose of property by a will.

By the middle of the 19th century in England, the *Married Women's Property Act, 1882*,[54] extended the concept of equitable separate property to any property owned by a married woman. In this way, a married woman was entitled by statute, to retain as separate property, that which she owned at the time of the marriage.

Where a gratuitous transfer of property is made from one person to another, the presumption in equity is of a resulting trust. Historically, gratuitous transfers from a husband to a wife gave rise to a presumption of advancement or gift, while gratuitous transfers from a wife to husband did not. Of course, either presumption could be rebutted with evidence to the contrary.[55]

Legislation in the three territories, Saskatchewan, Ontario and the Atlantic provinces eventually abolished the presumption of advancement between spouses. In Manitoba, however, the relevant legislation provides that the presumption of advancement does not apply to property acquired by either or both spouses before or after the marriage. The presumption does therefore continue to apply to property acquired during the marriage.[56]

A resulting trust can also arise from financial or other contributions to the acquisition of the property. In *Murdoch v. Murdoch*,[57] the Supreme Court of Canada considered this question when Irene Murdoch claimed beneficial ownership to half of the Alberta farm property to which her husband had legal title. The wife's evidence was that she worked in the fields, and handled machinery and livestock, doing everything that needed to be done around the ranch. In that case, Martland J, writing for the majority did not consider the wife's evidence, though undisputed by the husband, to be sufficient to give rise to a resulting trust.

---

[53] *Anger & Honsberger, ibid.*, footnote 48, Part V, c. 15.
[54] 1882, c. 75 (U.K.).
[55] *Anger & Honsberger, ibid.*, footnote 48, Part V.
[56] *Ibid.*
[57] (1973), 41 D.L.R. (3d) 367, [1975] 1 S.C.R. 423 [hereinafter *Murdoch*].

Subsequent case law concerning constructive trust has, however, led to different results. A constructive trust is another equitable remedy that can be used to go around legal title in order to redress unjust enrichment. The constructive trust remedy was first suggested by Laskin J. in his dissenting judgment in *Murdoch*, and was then taken up by another Supreme Court minority in *Rathwell v. Rathwell*,[58] and then by a majority in *Pettkus v. Becker*.[59]

The facts in *Pettkus*, briefly stated, were as follows. Pettkus and Becker never married. He had a successful bee-keeping business and she lived with him for about 20 years and contributed to the business. At the dissolution of the relationship, she sought a half-interest in the lands and a share in the bee-keeping business. At the trial level, the judge would not have acceded to her request on the basis that her work in the business was in the nature of risk capital (that is, based on the chance that he would marry her). On appeal, however, it was held that she was entitled to half of the business on the basis of constructive trust. The reasons for the decision were that while there was no resulting trust interest, since it was not possible to impute to Mr. Pettkus an intention, express or implied, to share his savings, Ms. Becker did have a constructive trust interest in half of the business because, as Wilson J. noted, "[t]he parties lived together as husband and wife, although unmarried, for almost twenty years during which period she not only made possible the acquisition of their first property in Franklin Centre by supporting them both exclusively from her income during 'the lean years', but worked side by side with him for 14 years building up the bee-keeping operation which was their main source of livelihood". The Supreme Court endorsed this reason for imposing a constructive trust interest.[60]

The requirements for establishing a constructive trust interest, as set out in *Rathwell* and *Pettkus* are as follows:

(i)   benefit;
(ii) corresponding deprivation;
(iii) absence of juristic reason for the enrichment; and
(iv) a causal connection between the benefit and deprivation.[61]

---

[58] (1978), 83 D.L.R. (3d) 289, [1978] 2 S.C.R. 436 [hereinafter *Rathwell*].

[59] (1980), 117 D.L.R. (3d) 257, [1980] 2 S.C.R. 834 [hereinafter *Pettkus*].

[60] *Supra*, at p. 265, quoting from the Court of Appeal judgment reported at (1978), 87 D.L.R. (3d) 101 at p. 104, 20 O.R. (2d) 105.

[61] A. Warner La Forest, *Anger & Honsberger Law of Real Property*, 3rd ed., looseleaf (Toronto: Canada Law Book, October, 2008), Part V, ch. 15.

The Supreme Court of Canada's decision in *Sorochan v. Sorochan*,[62] significantly extended the scope of the constructive trust remedy by allowing that a spouse without title to property could establish an interest on the basis of contributions to property that was acquired prior to the start of any intimate relationship. In *Sorochan*, the couple in question never married but lived together for 42 years, during which time they jointly worked a farming operation and had six children. She looked after the household and children and also worked long hours on the farm, for which she received no remuneration. When they started living together, he owned the land. In that case, the Court held that the three conditions for constructive trust had been met:

(i) the husband was enriched by the wife's work for which he did not provide remuneration. Through her work, the farm was maintained and preserved as valuable;

(ii) the years of labour constituted a corresponding deprivation to the wife; and

(iii) there was no juristic reason for the enrichment.

The wife had prejudiced herself with the reasonable expectation of receiving something in return for her efforts, and the husband had freely accepted the benefits where he knew or ought to have known of that reasonable expectation. Turning to the remedy, the Court found that there was a causal connection between the wife's labour, which directly and substantially contributed to the maintenance and preservation of the farm preventing asset deterioration or divestment, and the property. It was further held that monetary damages were inadequate since the wife had a reasonable expectation of actual interest in the property and the husband was or reasonably ought to have been aware of that expectation. The Court also noted that longevity of the relationship worked in favour of a constructive trust remedy.

In both *Pettkus*, and *Sorochan*, the Court noted that the contributions of the wives went well beyond the ordinary.

The majority decision in *Peter v. Beblow*,[63] placed certain limits on the ambit of the constructive trust doctrine by emphasizing the requirement of a direct connection between the contribution and the property on which the claim is being made, as well as highlighting that

---

[62] (1986), 29 D.L.R. (4th) 1, [1986] 2 S.C.R. 38 [hereinafter *Sorochan*].
[63] (1993), 101 D.L.R. (4th) 621, [1993] 1 S.C.R. 980.

a constructive trust remedy is only available where monetary damages will not suffice. In spite of this restriction, however, the female partner in that case was awarded the entire interest in the marital home previously owned by her spouse.

In *Peter v. Beblow*, the couple had cohabited for 12 years during which time she did most of the household work and looked after both her own and his children. He worked outside the house, saved money which he used to pay off the mortgage on the family home, buy a houseboat and a car. She managed to save up a bit of money and buy some property. She eventually left because of his drinking and abuse. The issue in that case was whether the Court could find a constructive trust interest despite the fact that she had managed to acquire some kind of property and contributed through household work rather than helping to run a business, as in the previous decisions on point. The Supreme Court found that indeed, she was entitled to a 100% interest in the house by way of constructive trust. The reason for this decision was that there was clearly unjust enrichment:

(i)   there was a benefit to him in the form of her domestic services;

(ii)   there was a corresponding deprivation to her because she was not compensated for these services;

(iii) there was also no obligation existing between the parties, and so no juristic reason for his enrichment at her expense.

The Court also decided that a constructive trust interest was the right remedy here because monetary compensation was inadequate, taking into account the likelihood that a monetary award would be paid, as well as the special interest in the property. A link between the services rendered and the property in which the trust was claimed was also found. As for quantum, the Court opined that the value of the trust is to be determined on the basis of the actual value of the matrimonial property — the "value survived" approach. It reflects the Court's best estimate of what is fair, having regard to the contribution which the claimant's services have made to the value surviving, bearing in mind the practical difficulty of calculating, with mathematical precision the value of particular contributions to the family property.

Since *Peter v. Beblow*, courts have been quite willing, particularly in British Columbia, to award constructive trust interests upon the termination of common-law relationships.[64] In most cases, however,

---

[64]   See, *e.g.*, *Dorflinger v. Melanson* (1994), 91 B.C.L.R. (2d) 91, 3 R.F.L. (4th) 261

the untitled spouse is awarded less than a half-share in the assets. Constructive trusts remain a very uncertain area of the law with the question outstanding as to whether courts will try to duplicate for common-law couples the approach under marital property regimes, or whether they will adopt a stricter approach, presuming significance to the absence of a formal marriage.

It nevertheless remains difficult to make out a claim of unjust enrichment where the title-holding spouse has paid the other spouse for the household services, or where the claiming spouse has his or her own financial or career independence.[65]

An unmarried cohabitant who has rendered household or child-care services may alternatively be entitled to reasonable compensation for the services, either pursuant to a contract or in an action for *quantum meruit*. Although the doctrine of unjust enrichment has most frequently been applied to unmarried cohabitants who have claimed a share of the value of the family home on the breakdown of the cohabiting relationships, it has also been applied to enable a 'common-law wife' to share her 'husband's' pension. See for example *Maloney v. Maloney*.[66]

Marriage and Statutory Rights and Obligations

As a social status, marriage leads to a whole basket of entitlements prescribed by legislation. Some of the more notable among these are discussed in this section.

(1) Family Law Act

For the purposes of Part I of the *FLA*, which deals with family property, the definition of "spouse" is restricted to either of two persons who are married to each other or have together entered into a marriage that is voidable or void, in good faith on the part of a person relying on this clause to assert any right.

For the purposes of Part III of the *FLA*, which deals with support obligations, the definition of "spouse" is broadened so as to include in addition either of two persons who are not married to each other and have cohabited either continuously for a period of not less than three years, or in a relationship of some permanence, if they are

---

(C.A.); *Mariano v. Manchisi* (1994), 4 E.T.R. (2d) 230, 8 R.F.L. (4th) 7 (Ont. Ct. (Gen. Div.)).

[65] *Ibid.*, footnote 61.

[66] (1993), 109 D.L.R. (4th) 161, 44 A.C.W.S. (3d) 319 (Ont. Div. Ct.).

the natural or adoptive parents of a child. Co-habiting spouses are therefore excluded from the application of the *FLA* with respect to claims of equalization and property but not for claims of support.

The underlying objective of the *FLA* is to ensure that on marriage breakdown or death each spouse will receive a fair share, which will usually be an equal share, of the value of assets accumulated during the course of the marriage.

Property claims between spouses are not running accounts, but rather crystallize only on the "valuation date". The valuation date is defined as the earlier of the following dates:

1. The date the spouses separate and there is no reasonable prospect that they will resume cohabitation.
2. The date a divorce is granted.
3. The date the marriage is declared a nullity.
4. The date one of the spouses commences an application based on improvident depletion that is subsequently granted.
5. The date before the date on which one of the spouses dies leaving the other spouse surviving.

The spouse holding the lesser net value of family property has a claim against the spouse holding the greater net family property. This claim is for one-half the difference between their respective net family properties, which when paid, has the effect of equalizing the spouses' net family property as at the date of separation. Hence it is known as the "equalization payment". Variation of the claim for one-half of the difference can be pled, but is rarely achieved in the absence of fraud or other unconscionable circumstances.

With the Royal Assent of Bill 133, *Family Statute Law Amendment Act*, on May 14th, 2009, the definition of net family property has been amended to add that debts and liabilities related directly to the acquisition of significant improvement of a matrimonial home are not to be deducted from the net family property calculation. Net family property is now defined as the value of all the property, except property described in subsection (2) [namely, excluded property], that a spouse owns on the valuation date, after deducting:

(a) the spouse's debts and other liabilities, including, for greater certainty, any contingent tax liabilities in respect of the property, and

(b) the value of property, other than a matrimonial home, that the spouse owned on the date of the marriage, after deducting the spouse's debts and other liabilities, *other than debts or liabilities related directly to the acquisition or significant improvement of a matrimonial home, calculated as of the date of the marriage* [emphasis added].

Property that is excluded from the valuation of the net family property is as follows:

(i) property, other than a matrimonial home, that was acquired by gift or inheritance from a third person after the date of the marriage;

(ii) income from such property;

(iii) damages or right to damages for personal injuries;

(iv) proceeds or a right to proceeds of a life insurance policy;

(v) property, other than a matrimonial home, into which property referred to in the previously listed items can be traced;

(vi) property that the spouses have agreed by a domestic contract is excluded from net family property. With the new legislation, debts and liabilities directly related to the acquisition or significant improvement of the matrimonial home are also deducted from the net family property calculation.

Where one spouse dies, marital status also entitles a married spouse to elect under the *FLA* whether to 'take' property under an existing will or to receive the entitlement under s. 5 of the *FLA*, which provides for the equalization of net properties. Similarly, when a spouse dies intestate, the surviving married spouse shall elect to receive the entitlement under Part II of the *Succession Law Reform Act*[67] ("*SLRA*") or to receive the entitlement under s. 5 of the *FLA*.

The *SLRA*, like the *FLA*, defines "spouses" as either of two persons who, (a) are married to each other, or (b) have together entered into a marriage that is voidable or void, in good faith on the part of the person asserting a right under this *FLA*.

Part II of the *SLRA* provides that where a person dies intestate in respect of property and is survived by a spouse and not survived by issue, the spouse is entitled to the property absolutely.[68]

Where a person dies intestate in respect of property having a net value of not more than the preferential share and is survived by a

---

[67] R.S.O. 1990, c. S.26.

[68] *Ibid.*, s. 44.

spouse and issue, the spouse is entitled to the property absolutely. Where a person dies intestate in respect of property having a net value of more than the preferential share and is survived by a spouse and issue, the spouse is entitled to the preferential share absolutely.[69]

The preferential share is defined as the amount prescribed by regulation. The preferential share is currently prescribed as $200,000. Both on marriage breakdown and upon death, marital status accordingly has very significant consequences for property division and testate or intestate succession.

(2) Divorce Reform

Divorce was not available in Upper Canada until 1930, so women had few options when they were married to an abusive or absent husband. In order to alleviate some of the hardship this created, the Court of Chancery was given jurisdiction to award alimony in 1837, but only when the wife could prove adultery, cruelty, or desertion of more than two years. Even when alimony was awarded however, it was often difficult to collect.

Concurrent with the property reforms set out above, were changes to the process of obtaining a divorce in Canada. Ontario brought in fault-based divorce similar to England's *Matrimonial Causes Act*[70] of 1857, with the passage of the *Divorce Act (Ontario) 1930*.[71] Men needed to show adultery to divorce their wives; wives needed to show adultery, rape, sodomy, bestiality, or bigamy. Canada's first federal divorce legislation, the *Divorce Act*,[72] included both fault and no-fault grounds for divorce. The latter allowed for a divorce after the parties had been living separate and apart for a period in excess of three years, irrespective of fault or cause of marriage breakdown. The *Divorce Act* was reformed in 1986, limiting the fault grounds to adultery and cruelty. The no-fault ground of separation was reduced to a period of only one year.

This chapter has explored the legal consequences of marriage from a historical perspective. It is only in this context that the application of an appropriate standard for capacity to marry can be developed.

---

[69]   *Ibid.*, s. 45.
[70]   20 & 21 Vict., c. 85.
[71]   S.C. 1930, c.14.
[72]   S.C. 1968, c. 24.

CHAPTER 4

TESTAMENTARY FREEDOM

This chapter is devoted to the concept of testamentary freedom. If we are to understand the current distinction that the law draws between capacity to make a will and capacity to marry, we must know what motivates both the freedoms and restrictions relating to these concepts.

Introduction

In Ontario, an individual is free to disinherit his or her children or grandchildren for any or no reason. This is true regardless of the age of the disinherited child or grandchild. As we will see below, however, dependants do have the option to apply for support, and so to circumvent disinheritance indirectly.

This is a contrast to civil law and Commonwealth jurisdictions where descendants are generally entitled to a specific share of the estate unless there are grounds for disinheritance. In Austria, for example, the child is entitled to one-half the amount he or she would have inherited under the intestacy rules unless the child was:

(i)   convicted of a crime and sentenced to 20 years or more as punishment;

(ii) committed an offence against the testator that involved intent and was punishable by more than a year of imprisonment; or

(iii) grossly neglected duties of care and support to the testator when the testator was in a position of need.

As another example, Louisiana reserved a certain portion of the estate, called the legitime, for qualified children and other lineal descendants entitled to take by representation. In order to merit disentitlement in Louisiana, one must:

(i)   injure, cruelly treat, or attempt to kill a parent;

(ii) unjustly accuse a parent of a serious crime (one punishable by life imprisonment or death);

(iii) commit a serious crime;

(iv) interfere with the parent's attempt to make a will;

(v) marry while a minor without the parent's permission;

(vi) fail to communicate with the parent for two years without just cause after attaining the age of majority and knowing how to contact the parent.

Without the presence of one of these factors, a child is entitled to the legitime. Furthermore, grounds for disinheritance may be challenged by the disinherited child after the parent's death, though the burden of proof lies with the challenging child. Changes to the legislation made in 1995, however, allow a testator to disinherit a child over age 24.

Limits to testamentary freedom exist in the form of the doctrine of undue influence, challenging mental capacity, and fraud and duress. A couple of articles published in the 1990s suggested that the courts will use the doctrine of undue influence to reverse testamentary dispositions that do not provide for the 'natural' objects of affection.[1]

Those who prefer limitations on testamentary freedom in order to benefit close family argue as follows:

> [F]orced heirship, an institution tested through the ages, remains a sound social policy to date because it helps preserve and strengthen the family by reminding parents of their societal responsibilities, and by binding family members together through life and beyond . . . [O]ther states are now beginning to realize that the rampant disintegration of the family is not unrelated to legal institutions that prompted a selfish individualism by glorifying the unrestricted freedom of testation.[2]

Others have associated testamentary freedom with, "the weakening of bonds of kinship, love, and friendship in cultural life" and the disregard for the special and natural bond between parent and child.[3]

Historical Backdrop

Historically, the progression in the common law has been from automatic inheritance entitlements to testamentary freedom. In the

---

[1] See, *e.g.*, M.B. Leslie, "The Myth of Testamentary Freedom" (1996), 38 Ariz. L. Rev. 235, at pp. 236-37, 245-46.

[2] K. Shaw Spaht, "Forced Heirship Changes: The Regrettable 'Revolution' Completed" (1996), 57 L.A. L. Rev. 55.

[3] See, *e.g.*, V.D. Rougeau, "No Bonds but those Freely Chosen: An Obituary for the Principle of Forced Heirship in American Law" (2008), 1 Civ. L. Comment, No. 3.

original laws of England, inheritance was governed by the rule of 'primogeniture', providing that all of a father's qualified land was to be automatically inherited by his eldest son. This rule was brought to England by Norman conquerors:

> From the perspective of the king, primogeniture considerably simplified the problem of deciding whose homage to receive at the death of a tenant-in-chief. At the end of the reign of Henry II (d. 1189), the principle was limited to land held by knight-service or military tenure, but the common law subsequently extended it to most free tenures. If one or more sons survived the decedent, the eldest son would inherit the land. Only if no son survived the decedent would the decedent's daughters have a claim, and in that case they would all take as coparceners. However, by the reign of Edward I (1272-1307), a rule had developed that if the eldest son predeceased the decedent leaving children of his own, any younger sons of the decedent would not take; rather the eldest son's children would take instead.[4]

Entirely different rules applied however to personal property. Jurisdiction for personal property fell within the domain of the ecclesiastical courts, which honoured the making of wills. Even here, though, the legitime was enforced, a custom adopted from Roman law, which required certain shares of personal property to go to the spouse or children. The ecclesiastical Church treated sons and daughters on par and also did not give preference to elder children.[5]

The rule of primogeniture was unpopular for a number of reasons, including the feudal tax that it attracted. In 1536, under King Henry VIII, Parliament passed the *Statute of Uses*, which transferred legal title of all land held in use from the feoffees to the beneficiaries. The *Statute of Wills* in 1540 created the right to dispose of land by will. The statute still protected one-third of the land for the descendants' heirs (the legitime), but the land owner was free to dispose of the rest of his property by will. Gradually the legitime passed into obscurity and by the end of the 1500s, it had disappeared in most parts of England. By the end of the 1800s it had disappeared altogether in England.[6]

Testamentary freedom, or the ability to disinherit was therefore a reaction to this original constraint. In particular, children who were

---

[4]   J.C. Tate, "Caregiving and the Case for Testamentary Freedom" (2008), 42 U.C. Davis L. Rev. 129, at pp. 149-50.

[5]   *Ibid.*, at pp. 145-52.

[6]   *Ibid.*, at pp. 152-56.

not the eldest were motivated to seek reform to the original inheritance structure.

Policy Reasons for Testamentary Freedom

An often-heard justification for testamentary freedom is that by allowing a testator to choose how his or her wealth will be distributed after death, hard work and savings are encouraged throughout each individual's lifetime.

Another argument is that testamentary freedom is simply in line with the value placed by North American culture on individualism. Any laws enforcing certain inheritance rules would be a form of restriction on personal choice and therefore incommensurate with the value placed by our culture on such choice. It is worth noting, though, that the law does in most cases restrict a spouse's right to disinherit his or her spouse. Where a spouse dies leaving a will, the surviving spouse may either elect to take under the will or to receive his or her equalization entitlement under s. 5 of the *Family Law Act*.[7] In Ontario, if a spouse dies intestate, there is currently a legislated preferential share of $200,000 to which the surviving spouse is at minimum entitled.[8]

John Langbein has argued that the nature of wealth-transmission changed dramatically over the 20th century. While prior to the 20th century, wealth transfer was usually in the form of the family farm or firm, this was transformed into the transfer of skills from parent to child in the 20th century. Educational expenses therefore became the main form of wealth transfer for the middle classes, exacerbated by the fact that with parents living longer, there was usually less to transfer after death.[9]

If Langbein is right, then testamentary freedom is unobjectionable since children have already received the bulk of their inheritance-entitlement well before their parents die.

In fact, there are those who argue that devising property to one's children should be discouraged since it only accentuates the divide between the rich and the poor. That is, it is argued that those fortunate enough to have been raised and educated by wealthy parents have no

---

[7] R.S.O. 1990, c. F. 3.

[8] Tate, *ibid.*, footnote 4, at pp. 156-63.

[9] J.H. Langbein, "The Twentieth Century Revolution in Family Wealth Transmission" (1988), 86 Mich. L. Review 722, at pp. 722-24.

need for or deserve of an additional wealth windfall from their parents upon death.[10]

Reward for eldercare services is another reason to allow testamentary freedom. That is, testamentary freedom allows a parent to reward the child or children who take care of him or her in their twilight years. This freedom also allows the elderly, however, to reward an unfairly favoured child or to reward non-related caregivers, and to potentially become the victims of predators striving to persuade them to disinherit their children in their favour.

An aging population means that children are called upon and will be increasingly called upon to take care of their elderly parents for longer periods of time. This responsibility can come at the expense of career and attendant financial benefits. It is also the case that women bear this responsibility disproportionately to men.[11] Given this reality, the freedom of the testator to financially reward one child who has provided the bulk of the support in the testator's later years can be seen as beneficial.

Research shows that where testators opt for unequal division of assets, this division often favours children who have or are expected to provide the bulk of the elder care. Other research, however, indicates that 70-83% of parents choose equal division of property in their bequests to their children.[12]

Limitations on Freedoms

Of course the greatest potential limit on testamentary freedom is the ability of a dependant to seek support from the estate of a deceased individual. This remedy is available where an individual was formerly supported by the testator such that the testator had an on-going duty to provide support, but failed to do so by way of bequest. The first dependant support provision was enacted in Ontario in 1929. Although the primary purpose of the legislation is to ensure that dependants are provided for, it is also instrumental in sparing the state from the burden of supporting individuals who were previously supported by a private individual.

---

[10] M.L. Ascher, "Curtailing Inherited Wealth" (1990), 89 Mich. L. Review 69, at p. 90.

[11] See *e.g.*, National Alliance for Caregiving & Zogby Int'l, Miles Away; The MetLife Study of Long-distance Caregiving 2 (2004), available online at: www.caregiving.org/data/milesaway.pdf (accessed December 3, 2009).

[12] E.C. Norton and D.H. Taylor, "Equal Division of Estates and the Exchange Motive" (2005), 17 J. Aging & Soc. Pol'y 63, at p. 74.

Entitlement to support is available to non-married spouses and the *Succession Law Reform Act*[13] also treats all children, whether the product of a marital relationship or not, and whether or not they are adopted, as equal.

The Rule against Perpetuities imposes another kind of limit in stating that no interest is valid unless it must vest indefeasibly within a certain period of time (the traditional perpetuity period being "a life in being plus 21 years"). If at the time the interest becomes effective, whether by virtue of an *inter vivos* transfer or by operation of a will, and it is clear that it will not vest indefeasibly within the perpetuity period, the interest is deemed a nullity and the intended gift will fail. If this occurs with respect to the residue of a testator's estate and there is no alternate distribution provision, the residue goes out as on an intestacy. (The rule does not apply to trusts established for the benefit of charities, such trusts being permitted to exist "in perpetuity").

Testamentary Capacity

The law on testamentary capacity is reasonably well-established. This given, the main challenge in cases involving questions of testamentary capacity is to establish facts so that the settled legal principles may properly be applied to them. In *Banks v. Goodfellow*,[14] Cockburn J. defined the legal test for testamentary capacity as follows (this passage was also quoted by Cullity J. in *Banton v. Banton*,[15] a case that will be discussed in greater detail in a later chapter):

> It is essential to the exercise of such a power [the power of testamentary freedom] that a testator shall understand the nature of the act and its effects; shall understand the extent of the property of which he is disposing; shall be able to comprehend and appreciate the claims to which he ought to give effect; and, with a view to the latter object, that no disorder of the mind shall poison his affections, pervert his sense of right, or prevent the exercise of his natural faculties — that no insane delusion shall influence his will in disposing of his property and bring about a disposal of it which, if the mind had been sound, would not have been made.[16]

---

[13]   R.S.O. 1990, c. S.26.

[14]   (1870), L.R. 5 Q.B. 549, at p. 565.

[15]   (1998), 164 D.L.R. (4th) 176, 66 O.T.C. 161 (Gen. Div.), supp. reasons 164 D.L.R. (4th) at p. 244, 83 A.C.W.S. (3d) 531 (Gen. Div.).

[16]   *Supra*, at p. 196.

This chapter has set out the law relating to testamentary freedom. This will assist us in the chapters that follow to appreciate the distinctions made in current case law between testamentary capacity and the capacity to marry, and the consequences thereof.

CHAPTER 5

CAPACITY TO MARRY

This chapter addresses the core subject of our inquiry, the capacity to marry. Marriage is a central societal institution. Society strives to encourage marriage for the purposes of stability and child-rearing. The law places certain limited controls on marriage, such as a minimum capacity requirement for an individual to enter into a marital unit. The focus of this investigation is the definition and interpretation of this requirement. In particular, we argue that the requirement may be too lenient given the profound consequences that attend marriage. One particular area of concern is with so-called predatory marriages that take advantage of a person with limited capacity. That is, given the property status-enhancing consequences of marriage, those with impaired capacity may be convinced to marry so that their spouse may achieve these desirable benefits. In this chapter, we discuss the basic requirements for capacity to marry, the idea of good faith, the possibility of forced marriages, as well as marriage contracts.

Basic Requirements

Capacity to marry may exist despite incapacity in other legal matters. The requirements of legal capacity vary significantly as between different areas of law, and must be applied specifically to the particular act or transaction that is in issue. Progressive tests for capacity are decision based. As a result, a person may lack testamentary capacity, yet have the capacity to marry. Similarly, a person may be capable of marrying despite having been declared mentally incompetent and having had a property guardian or guardian of the person appointed.

The law prescribes a different standard of capacity in different contexts. Contexts in which capacity is required include the following:

1. giving instructions for and to execute a will or trust, in other words: "testamentary capacity";[1]

2. making other testamentary dispositions;[2]
3. contracting;[3]
4. managing property;[4]
5. managing personal care;[5]
6. granting or revoking a Continuing Power of Attorney for Property;[6]
7. granting or revoking a Power of Attorney for Personal Care;[7]
8. consenting to treatment decisions in accordance with the *Health Care Consent Act*;[8]
9. gifting or selling property;[9]
10. instructing a lawyer; and
11. marrying.

Capacity is *decision, time,* and *situation* specific. The relevant time period is the time at which the decision in issue is made. This definition of capacity also implies that legal capacity is fluid. There is a legal presumption of capacity unless and until the presumption is legally rebutted.[10]

---

[1] The test for testamentary capacity is set out in *Banks v. Goodfellow* (1870), L.R. 5 Q.B.; *Murphy v. Lamphier* (1914), 31 O.L.R. 287 at p. 318, [1914] O.J. No. 32 (QL) (Div. Ct.); and *Schwartz v. Schwartz* (1970), 10 D.L.R. (3d) 15, [1970] 2 O.R. 61 (C.A.), affd 20 D.L.R. (3d) 313, [1972] S.C.R. 150.

[2] The *Succession Law Reform Act*, R.S.O. 1990, c. S. 26, s. 1, as amended, defines a will as follows:
    "will" includes,
        (a) a testament,
        (b) a codicil,
        (c) an appointment by will or by writing in the nature of a will in exercise of a power, and
        (d) any other testamentary disposition. ("testament").

[3] *Hart v. O'Connor*, [1985] A.C. 1000 (P.C.).

[4] The *Substitute Decisions Act, 1992*, S.O. 1992, c. 30, s. 6, as amended.

[5] *Ibid.*, s. 45.

[6] *Ibid.*, s. 8.

[7] *Ibid.*, s. 47.

[8] *Health Care Consent Act, 1996*, S.O. 1996, c. 2, Sch. A, s. 41.

[9] *Archer v. St. John* (2008), 84 Alta. L.R. (4th) 249, 439 A.R. 260 (Q.B), supp. reasons 88 Alta. L.R. (4th) 152, 439 A.R. 275 (Q.B.); *Pecore v. Pecore* (2007), 279 D.L.R. (4th) 513, [2007] 1 S.C.R. 795; *Beaney (Deceased) (Re)*, [1978] 2 All E.R. 595, [1978] 1 W.L.R. 770 at p. 774 (Ch. D.); *Morris (Deceased), Special trustees for Great Ormond Street Hospital for Children v. Pauline Rushin*, [2000] All E.R. (D) 598 (Ch. D.).

[10] *Palahnuk v. Palahnuk Estate*, [2006] O.J. No. 5304 (QL), 154 A.C.W.S. (3d) 996 (S.C.J.) [hereinafter *Palahnuk Estate*]; *Brillinger v. Brillinger-Cain*, [2007] O.J.

(1)   Decision-Specific

Capacity is decision-specific in that, as determined by the legislation, the capacity to grant a power of attorney for property differs from the capacity to grant a power of attorney for personal care, which differs from the capacity to manage one's property or personal care. Testamentary capacity, the capacity to marry and the capacity to enter into a contract involve different considerations as determined at common law.

(2)   Time-Specific

Capacity is time-specific in that legal capacity can fluctuate over time. That is, the legal standard allows for 'good' and 'bad' days where capacity is concerned. Obviously, an otherwise capable person may lack capacity when he or she is under the influence of alcohol. Even where an individual suffers from a condition that is non-reversible, unremitting, or even involves a progressive decline, his or her legal status with respect to capacity can vary.

The Ontario Court of Appeal affirmed the decision in *Knox v. Burton*,[11] establishing that a cognitively impaired person can fluctuate between being capable and incapable of granting a power of attorney.

In this decision, three expert assessor opinions were sought to establish whether the grantor had capacity to grant a power of attorney for property. In 2004, at the time of the trial, Mrs. Knox was 80 years old. She had granted a continuing power of attorney to her son in May 1999. In December 2002, she had been described by one geriatric psychiatrist as having "progressive cognitive decline suggestive of a dementing process that mildly interfered with her occupational and social functioning". One of the assessors found her incapable while the other two found her capable. The first assessor met Mrs. Knox on February 7, 2003 and found her incapable of granting or revoking a continuing power of attorney. The second assessor met with her 17 days later and found her capable in these regards. A third assessor found Mrs. Knox also capable upon meeting with her on April 24, 2003. A new continuing power of attorney for property was granted by Mrs. Knox to her nephew on May 2, 2003.

No. 2451 (QL), 158 A.C.W.S. (3d) 482 (S.C.J.); *Knox v. Burton* (2004), 6 E.T.R. (3d) 285, 130 A.C.W.S. (3d) 216 (Ont. S.C.J.).

[11]   *Supra*, footnote 10.

At the trial, the third assessor testified and explained that she had read the assessments of both of the other assessors. The trial judge accepted the evidence, relied on the presumption of capacity, and found that in light of the evidence of the two assessors who found Mrs. Knox capable, the presumption of capacity had not been rebutted.

When the Court of Appeal affirmed this decision, they addressed the appellants with respect to fluctuating capacity as follows

> We also do not agree that the evidence that Mrs. Knox's capacity could fluctuate necessitated any shifting of the onus of proof. The appellant had the legal onus. The potential variability of Mrs. Knox's condition was one feature of the evidence. It was specifically addressed by Dr. Munson in his [sic] evidence. The trial judge accepted Dr. Munson's evidence as she was entitled to do.[12]

More recently, in *Palahnuk Estate*[13] and *Brillinger v. Brillinger-Cain*,[14] Ontario courts have referred to *Knox v. Burton*[15] for the proposition that the capacity of a testator may be variable over time.

Assessing capacity is an imperfect science which further complicates the determination. Lay evidence as well as professional and expert evidence can be determinative in certain circumstances. The standard of assessment varies — this too, is seen as a hurdle.

Both *Grav (Re)*[16] and *Palahnuk Estate* suggest that expert opinion need not be definitive where capacity is concerned. Given that capacity may be variable over time, expert examinations or assessments that do not state when the incapacity occurred, or are not contemporaneous with the giving of instructions, may be less probative than the evidence of a drafting solicitor who applies the legal test for capacity at the time that the instructions are received.

(3) Situation-Specific

Lastly, capacity is situation-specific in that the choices that a person makes in granting a power of attorney or making a will affect a court's determination of capacity. For example, if a mother appoints her eldest child as power of attorney, this choice will be viewed with less suspicion and concern for potential diminished capacity than if she appoints her recently-hired gardener for the same purpose.

---

[12] (2005), 14 E.T.R. (3d) 27, 137 A.C.W.S. (3d) 1076 (Ont. C.A.), at para. 2.
[13] *Supra*, footnote 10.
[14] *Supra*, footnote 10.
[15] *Supra*, footnote 10.
[16] (2007), 35 E.T.R. (3d) 193, 155 A.C.W.S. (3d) 959 (B.C.S.C.).

Void or Voidable Marriages

Where the requisite capacity is present, another basis upon which a marriage may be set aside is undue influence. Where there is a finding of undue influence, a person is found not to have exercised his or her own volition and the actions taken by the person in writing a will, granting a power of attorney, and so on, may be undermined. It is in this way that undue influence provides grounds for finding a will invalid. An allegation of undue influence requires proof of coercion. Undue influence in the context of contracts or other transactions may be proved not only by evidence of actual undue influence but also by way of the doctrine of presumed undue influence.[17]

There are two key elements required to establish undue influence:

1. a relationship of influence between the parties; and
2. a transaction that calls for explanation. If a relationship of trust and confidence is established and the transaction is such that an explanation is called for, a presumption of undue influence arises. The onus is then shifted to the defendant who must demonstrate that the donor entered into the matter with his or her will unconstrained.[18]

Undue influence is explained as follows:

1. influence which overbears the will of the person influenced, so that in truth, what the person does is not his or her own act;
2. the ability to dominate the will of the grantor/donor/testator;
3. the exertion of pressure so as to overbear the volition and the wishes of a testator;[19] and
4. the inappropriate use of power by one person over another to induce action.[20]

---

[17] D. Goodman, B. Hall, P. Hewitt, H. Labes and H. Mason, *Probate Disputes and Remedies*, 2nd ed. (Bristol: Jordans, 2008), at pp. 6-7.

[18] *Ibid.*, at p. 7; and *Royal Bank of Scotland plc v. Etridge (No 2)*, [2002] 2 A.C. 773, [2001] UKHL 44.

[19] *Dmyterko (Litigation Guardian of) v. Kulikowsky* (1992), 47 E.T.R. 66, 35 A.C.W.S. (3d) 755 (Ont. Ct. (Gen. Div.)) [hereinafter *Dmyterko*]; *Leger v. Poirier*, [1944] 3 D.L.R. 1, [1944] S.C.R. 152 at pp. 161-62 [hereinafter *Leger*].

[20] *Longmuir v. Holland* (2000), 192 D.L.R. (4th) 62, 81 B.C.L.R. (3d) 99 (C.A.); *Keljanovic Estate v. Sanseverino* (2000), 186 D.L.R. (4th) 481, 34 E.T.R. (2d) 32 (Ont. C.A.), leave to appeal to S.C.C. refused 192 D.L.R. (4th) vii, 143 O.A.C. 398*n sub nom. Keljanovic Estate (Re)*; *Berdette v. Berdette*, [1991] O.J. No 3221 (QL) (C.A.); *Brandon v. Brandon*, [2001] O.T.C. 571, 107 A.C.W.S. (3d) 142 (S.C.J.), revd in part 6 E.T.R. (3d) 210, 127 A.C.W.S. (3d) 549 (C.A.), leave to

In addition, the timing, circumstances and magnitude of the result of the undue influence may be sufficient to prove undue influence in certain circumstances.[21] This is particularly the case in the context of victimization.[22]

In order to enter into marriage that can not be subsequently voided or declared a nullity, there must be a minimal understanding of the nature of the contract of marriage. No party is required to understand all the consequences of marriage.

As is often mentioned in marriage vows, marriage is intended to be exclusive, terminated only by death, and is founded on mutual support and cohabitation. At the time of marriage, parties often fail to consider the other facets of the marital union: an obligation to provide financial support; the enforced sharing of equity acquired during the marriage; and the resulting disposition of one's estate.

Classic English cases including the decision of *Durham v. Durham*[23] are often cited at the outset of the analysis in most subsequent cases dealing with claims to void or declare a marriage a nullity. *Durham* begins with the principal that,

> the contract of marriage is a very simple one, which does not require a high degree of intelligence to comprehend.[24]

It goes on to state that it includes

> . . . a capacity to understand the nature of the contract, and the duties and responsibilities which it creates.[25]

In other words, one must only be able to understand the basic nature of a marriage and its obligations and responsibilities.

The Canadian development of the law regarding the capacity to marry over the past 25 years is reasonably well-developed and consistent. Starting with *Lacey v. Lacey*,[26] we can see the interplay amongst the concepts of consent to marriage: the capacity to care for

---

appeal to S.C.C. refused [2004] 2 S.C.R. v, 197 O.A.C. 399*n*; *Lamoureux v. Craig* (1914), 17 D.L.R. 422, 49 S.C.R. 305; and *Hall v. Hall* (1868), L.R. 1 P & D.

[21] *Dmyterko, supra*, footnote 19; *Leger, supra*, footnote 19.

[22] *Allcard v. Skinner* (1887), 36 Ch. D. 145 (C.A.).

[23] (1885), 10 P.D. 80 [hereinafter *Durham*].

[24] *Supra*, at p. 82.

[25] *Supra*, at p. 82.

[26] [1983] B.C.J. No. 1016 (QL) (S.C.) [hereinafter *Lacey*].

one's self both financially and personally, the capacity to marry and the vitiation of marriage by operation of undue influence.

In *Lacey*, a 78-year-old man married one of his fellow nursing home companions, an 80-year-old woman, thus revoking a will which had named his only son as his beneficiary. Although both husband and wife demonstrated intermittent traits of dementia at the time of the marriage, according to the nursing home records and the Pastor who married them, they appeared to participate in, understand, and express enthusiasm for the marriage ceremony.

The marriage ceremony was public and celebrated by both families. The relationship deteriorated within months and the husband considered annulment of the marriage, but did not proceed. He did not draw a new will, even though he knew that his previous will, leaving everything to his only son had been revoked by the marriage. Justice Wong refused the son's petition to declare the marriage a nullity when the father died 11 months later, concluding that: "either the father did not wish to change the situation which he created, or Divine Providence did not intend that he do so".[27]

Because the marriage stood, an estate of $16,000 fell to the incapacitated wife for her care, rather than to the son. In his reasons, Wong J. quoted *Durham* with approval, and went on to say:

> Thus at law, the essence of a marriage contract is an engagement between a man and a woman to live together and to love one another as husband and wife to the exclusion of all others. It is a simple contract which does not require high intelligence to comprehend. It does not involve consideration of a large variety of circumstances required in other acts involving others, such as the making of a Will. In addition, the character of consent for this particular marriage did not involve consideration of other circumstances normally required by other persons contemplating marriage — such as establishing a source of income, maintaining a home, or contemplation of children.[28]

It is worthwhile to consider the implications of Wong J.'s comments on marriage in the above text. There may be some unfortunate consequences to allowing the particular circumstances of those entering into the marriage to govern the requisite level of capacity for consent.

In the 1998 Ontario case of *Banton v. Banton*[29] Cullity J. provided an overview of the development of the law in Canada and

---

[27] *Supra*, at para. 38.
[28] *Supra*, footnote 26, at para. 31.

51

stated that a party was only required to understand the nature and responsibilities of marriage. He contrasted the English courts' continued added requirement of being capable of understanding the nature of the contract itself, which included being capable of taking care of one's own person and property.[30] In the English development of the law, the ability to appreciate and manage property was a prerequisite to the capacity to enter marriage, which by its very act, created property rights.

Justice Cullity seemed swayed both by the lack of Canadian case law with this added requirement and by the fact that the *Substitute Decisions Act*[31] has now separated the ability to care for one's self and one's property. Justice Cullity thought it unfair to make the ability to care for one's property a requirement for marriage, especially for older persons who may well be able to live together in a married relationship but have their property taken care of through a power of attorney. Justice Cullity felt that incapacity as to property management alone should not invalidate a marriage. He acknowledged, however, that incapacity regarding both personal care and property may well be enough to find incapacity to marry.[32]

Nonetheless, Cullity J. declined to find the marriage a nullity, or to void it. He separated the issue of consent to marriage from that of capacity to marry, and analyzed each as a separate concept. One did not necessarily give rise to the other. Finding the husband to have consented and to have been a "willing victim" despite undue influence in his subsequent testamentary disposition was not sufficient to conclude that he was incapable of entering into the marriage.

The Alberta case of *Barrett Estate v. Dexter*[33] declared a 1996 marriage between the 93-year-old husband and the 54-year-old wife a nullity on the basis that a lack of capacity both in personal care and property was evidence of a lack of capacity to marry.

The facts leading to the finding were persuasive. The wife had taken increasing control of the husband's affairs while a tenant in his home, alienating him from the family and community supports that had previously sustained him. The wife secretly arranged the marriage, employing the limousine and taxi drivers as witnesses. She

---

[29] (1998), 164 D.L.R. (4th) 176, 66 O.T.C. 161 (Gen. Div.), supp. reasons 164 D.L.R. (4th) at p. 244, 83 A.C.W.S. (3d) 531 (Gen. Div.) [hereinafter *Banton*].

[30] *Supra,* at pp. 225-28 (D.L.R.).

[31] S.O. 1992, c. 30.

[32] *Supra*, footnote 29, at p. 228.

[33] (2000), 34 E.T.R. (2d) 1, 268 A.R. 101 (Q.B.) [hereinafter *Barrett Estate*].

then escalated her efforts by securing a letter of competence from an out-of-town physician and having the husband execute a handmade will leaving his estate of $1 million to the wife. A subsequent hospitalization occasioned by an injury to the husband resulted in a finding that he was severely cognitively impaired.

In his reasons, Wilkins J. quoted the test in *Durham* and then went on to summarize overwhelming medical evidence from three physicians that:

> Dwight [the husband] would not understand the nature of the contract; his relationship with his intended spouse; his previous marriage history; or the impact of his marriage on legal matters.[34]

Justice Wilkins found that the medical evidence was sufficient to establish that the husband lacked the mental capacity to marry the wife, to appreciate the consequences of the marriage to himself or to his children. The marriage was thus determined a nullity, without the need to void it or determine the claim of undue influence by the wife.

The issue returned to Ontario jurisprudence in the case of *Sung Estate (Re)*.[35] The facts in *Sung Estate* were in many ways similar to those in *Banton*. There was a discrepancy of age (the husband was 70 and the wife 47), the husband was severely mentally ill and unable to care for himself, the marriage was kept a secret from the husband's family, and the wife was in a position of influence.

Justice Greer found that the wife pressured the husband into marrying her by threatening to no longer care for him. She states that:

> There is no question that the form of marriage that Sung and Feng went through complies with the provincial statutory provisions of the *Marriages Act*. The question, however, is whether this marriage was *void ab initio*. It was not a voidable marriage, as neither party prior to Sung's death took steps to have it declared such. In *De Reneville v. De Reneville*, [1948] P. 100, Lord Greene M.R., stated the following at p. 111:
>
> "... a void marriage is one that will be regarded by every court in any case in which the existence of the marriage is in issue as never having taken place and can so be treated by both parties to it without the necessity of any decree annulling it: a voidable marriage is one that will be regarded by every court as a valid subsisting marriage until a

---

[34] *Supra,* at para. 78.

[35] (2003), 1 E.T.R. (3d) 296, 37 R.F.L. (5th) 441 *sub nom. Feng v. Sung Estate* (Ont. S.C.J.), affd 11 E.T.R. (3d) 169, 9 R.F.L. (6th) 229 *sub nom. Feng v. Sung Estate* (C.A.) [hereinafter *Sung Estate*].

> decree annulling it has been pronounced by a court of competent jurisdiction."
>
> There is a line of old English cases, which supports this finding. Later English cases under new statutory legislation have overridden the old common law principles making such marriages voidable but not *void ab initio*. That legislation is not applicable in Ontario, which is still governed by the old common law rules.
>
> I am satisfied on the evidence before me that the marriage of Sung and Feng was void *ab initio*.[36]

Justice Greer found the consent evidenced in *Banton* to be of a different nature as the husband had sufficient memory and understanding to continue to appreciate the nature and responsibilities of the relationship. The inability to care for himself and his property was not in itself sufficient to make him incapable of marriage.

Justice Greer cited with approval the *Barrett Estate* case, summarizing the relationship between undue influence and lack of capacity. In the case before her she stated:

> If I had not found that Sung was unduly influenced and coerced into his marriage with Feng, I am satisfied on the evidence that Sung lacked the mental capacity, as set out by Dr. Malloy,[37] *supra*, to enter the marriage.[38]

Justice Greer continues with a very helpful analysis of the role of undue duress as a ground for declaring a marriage a nullity. She contrasts the policy concern that marriages not be lightly set aside with the approach that:

> ... where duress is alleged as a ground for declaring an alleged marriage a nullity, it must be shown that there existed fear of sufficient degree to vitiate consent.[39]

The question remains, however, whether fear is a sufficient basis upon which a marriage ought to be nullified, or declared *void ab initio*.

The cases mentioned in this section are discussed in greater detail in the review of case law in Chapter 6, "Case Law Review".

---

[36] *Supra*, at paras. 51-53.
[37] The physician giving evidence in *Banton, supra*, footnote 29.
[38] *Sung Estate, supra*, footnote 35, at para. 62.
[39] *Sung Estate, supra*, footnote 35, at para. 65. See: W. Kent Power, *Power on Divorce and Other Matrimonial Causes*, 3d ed. (Toronto: Carswell, 1976-1980), Vol. II, at p. 81 (Sch. A).

Good Faith

A further point of entry regarding the capacity to marry is found through the requirement of entering a marriage in good faith, as set out in the definition of spouse in the *Family Law Act*[40] ("*FLA*"). Spouse is defined in s. 1(1) as:

> . . . either of two persons who,
> (a) are married to each other, or
> (b) have together entered into a marriage that is voidable or void, in good faith on the part of a person relying on this clause to assert any right.

Because this definition is specific to the *FLA* it can only be used as a remedy by those looking for relief under the *FLA*.

The issue of what it means to go through a void marriage in good faith was addressed in *Guptill v. Wilfred*.[41] There, the parties had married when the husband was still married to his first wife, which was not disclosed to his second wife. The husband stated that he believed he was divorced from his first wife at the time he married the second, and he therefore entered into the marriage in good faith. The court found otherwise.

Justice Warner referenced three Ontario cases that dealt with the issue of good faith, finding that the cases stood for the idea that "only the spouse who knew that the marriage was flawed was not a 'spouse'".[42]

In *Guptill*, the husband had been able to obtain a marriage licence by stating on the application that he had never been married. He argued that because he met the formal requirements for marriage, he should be found to have entered the marriage in good faith.

Justice Warner found, however, that good faith means more than meeting the formal statutory requirements for marriage — it includes being "capable of entering into a valid marriage".[43] Upon discovering that the husband knew on the date of marriage that he was still married to his first wife, Warner J. found that the husband did not go through with the second marriage in good faith.[44]

---

[40] R.S.O. 1990, c. F.3.
[41] (2009), 66 R.F.L. (6th) 129, 275 N.S.R. (2d) 170 (S.C.) [hereinafter *Guptill*].
[42] *Supra*, at para. 21.
[43] *Supra*, at para. 28.
[44] *Supra*, at para. 64.

Forced Marriage

A forced marriage occurs where people are coerced into marriage against their will or under duress. Duress can include both physical and emotional pressure.[45] Forced marriages are often perpetrated by parents to maintain religious or cultural ideals, or to secure advantage through family alliances or foreign marriages.

Forced marriages are an international issue of increasing concern. They have been rightly characterized as exercises in human trafficking, violence and human rights violations. A number of countries, such as the United Kingdom, have Forced Marriage Units which provide awareness, education and assistance to those affected.

The United Nations took an early position on marriage within its Charter:

> No marriage shall be legally entered into without the full and free consent of both parties, such consent to be expressed by them in person after due publicity and in the presence of the authority competent to solemnize the marriage and of witnesses, as prescribed by law.[46]

The Charter is most instructive in the normative manner of marriage. Marriage is consensual, public, and duly entered into within prescribed laws. Signatory countries, inclusive of Canada, have undertaken to ensure that a prerequisite for all marriages within its jurisdiction is the free and informed consent of both parties.

Common law courts have expanded the finding of duress in forced marriage from that of physical coercion to emotional pressure. While "reluctant" or "resentful" consent may not amount to duress, if the will of the individual has been overborne by the circumstantial pressure, a finding of duress will void the marriage.[47] While Canada has not criminalized forced marriage, a number of countries such as Norway and Belgium, Australia and Germany have done so. In Canada, redress for a forced marriage is limited to the civil courts.

---

[45] *Annotated Bibliography on Comparative and International Law Relating to Forced Marriage*, Department of Justice Canada (August 2007), available online at: http://www.justice.gc.ca/eng/pi/fcy-fea/lib-bib/rep-rap/2007/mar/index.html#a01 (accessed December 3, 2009).

[46] Convention on Consent to Marriage, Minimum Age for Marriage and Registration of Marriages, Office of the High Commissioner for Human Rights. General Assembly Resolution 1763 A (XVII), November 7, 1962, entered into force 9 December, 1964.

[47] *Ibid.*, at p. 8.

The study of forced marriages to date has focused on female child marriages within religious constructs. In a forced marriage, a spouse is compelled to marry out of fear, duress, or violence. The situation of a senior who fears being alone and unable to care for him or herself can be analogous.

Capacity to Separate

There are at least two facets to an incapacitated individual's vulnerability in the context of marriage. The first relates, as already discussed, to the individual's capacity to marry and whether the act of marriage along with its attendant rights and responsibilities can be fully understood by the contracting spouse. The second is the capacity to separate and divorce in the event that the spouse is no longer content to remain in the marriage. Is the capacity to separate the same threshold as the capacity to marry? The question remains that if a person is unable to appreciate the risks and legal consequences resulting from marriage before entering into it, can he or she appreciate those risks afterwards? If so unable, pressure to leave the marriage would only arise from persons negatively affected by the marriage, such as prior caregivers and family members. Can the healthy (or predatory) spouse defeat an expression to separate as arising from duress?

In *Calvert (Litigation Guardian of) v. Calvert*,[48] the Ontario Court of Appeal discussed the capacity to separate in the following context. The appellant appealed from a judgment granting the respondent a divorce and awarding an equalization payment. The trial judge had rejected the appellant's argument that the respondent lacked the requisite mental capacity to form the intention to live separate and apart. The court held that the *Divorce Act* requirements were satisfied since: the respondent had the capacity to separate when the parties did so; the respondent, Mrs Calvert, did not waiver from her wish to remain separate and apart so long as she had capacity; and the period of separation was uninterrupted. That is, that the couple had lived separate and apart for at least one year prior to the determination of the divorce proceeding and were living separate and apart at the commencement of the proceeding. To require further proof of capacity at each point and for each relevant period would

---

[48] (1998), 37 O.R. (3d) 221, 106 O.A.C. 299 *sub nom. Calvert v. Calvert* (C.A.), leave to appeal to S.C.C. refused 111 O.A.C. 197*n sub nom. Calvert v. Calvert*, 228 N.R. 98*n*.

defeat the purpose of s. 8(3)(b)(i) of the *Divorce Act*[49] (*"DA"*) which states that for the purposes of s. 2(a):

> (b) a period during which spouses have lived separate and apart shall not be considered to have been interrupted or terminated
>
>> (i) by reason only that either spouse has become incapable of forming or having an intention to continue to live separate and apart or of continuing to live separate and apart of the spouse's own volition, if it appears to the court that separation would probably have continued if the spouse had not become so incapable . . .

A recent decision from the British Columbia Court of Appeal addresses the issue of a wife's capacity to form the intention of living separate and apart. In *B. (A.) v. D. (C.)*,[50] the husband appealed two interlocutory orders made in a divorce action commenced by his wife. The husband wished to preserve the marriage and, among other things, challenged the wife's capacity to form the intention to live separate and apart.

His basis for this concern was his belief that his wife may be suffering from a delusional disorder causing her to believe that he was being unfaithful and was persecuting her. The husband submitted that if his concerns were substantiated, his wife's delusional or false beliefs could not form the basis for an intention to live separate and apart.

In considering this issue, D. Smith J., speaking on behalf of the British Columbia Court of Appeal, endorsed an approach to capacity that respects the personal autonomy of the individual in making decisions about his or her life. Justice Smith conceded that there may be instances where the mental disability of an individual reaches a level of incapacity which prevents them from managing their own affairs and thereby impacts their capacity to form the intention to live separate and apart. It was found, however, that since the wife was admitted to be mentally competent, she had a higher level of capacity than what was required to form such an intention:

> In summary, disordered or delusional thinking which may con- tribute to an individual's intention to live separate and apart, does not diminish that individual's capacity to form that intention, provided it does not reach the level of incapacity that interferes with the ability to manage his or her own affairs and instruct counsel. In this case, there is

---

[49] R.S.C. 1985, c. 3 (2nd Supp.).

[50] (2009), 94 B.C.L.R. (4th) 38, 66 R.F.L. (6th) 237 (C.A.), leave to appeal to S.C.C. refused [2009] S.C.C.A. No. 287 (QL).

no probative value to the evidence the husband seeks to obtain by his R. 30(1) application as the wife admittedly has the higher level of capacity to manage her own affairs. As a result, the wife's mental condition, even if she was found to be suffering from delusional disorder, cannot be an issue in the proceeding.[51]

The capacity to form the intention to live separate and apart is discussed by Professor Gerald B. Robertson in *Mental Disability and the Law in Canada*,[52] as follows:

Where it is the mentally ill spouse who is alleged to have formed the intention to live separate and apart, the court must be satisfied that that spouse possessed the necessary mental capacity to form that intention. This is probably similar to capacity to marry, and involves an ability to appreciate the nature and consequences of abandoning the marital relationship.[53]

Capacity to Divorce

Section 8(1) of the *DA* does not speak of capacity, or intention to divorce, but rather states that, "A court of competent jurisdiction may, on application by either or both spouses, grant a divorce to the spouse or spouses on the ground that there has been a breakdown of the marriage". A breakdown of the marriage is then defined to be established in s. 8(2) where:

(a) the spouses have lived separate and apart for at least one year immediately preceding the determination of the divorce proceeding and were living separate and apart at the commencement of the proceeding; or

(b) the spouse against whom the divorce proceeding is brought has, since celebration of the marriage,
　　(i)　committed adultery, or
　　(ii)　treated the other spouse with physical or mental cruelty of such a kind as to render intolerable the continued cohabitation of the spouses.

It is later, in s. 8(3)(i) of the *DA*, that the period of living separate and apart is further defined as running uninterrupted even if "either spouse has become incapable of forming or having an intention to continue to live separate and apart . . . if it appears to the court that

---

[51]　*Supra*, at para. 36.
[52]　2nd ed. (Toronto: Carswell, 1994).
[53]　*Ibid.*, at p. 272.

the separation would probably have continued if the spouse had not become so incapable". This assumes that a spouse who makes an application for a divorce is capable of forming the intention to separate. Provided that a person has formed such an intention, subsequent periods in which the spouse loses capacity will not interrupt the one year period necessary to grant the divorce.

The reading of the *DA* is unclear. It appears that provided an application has been made and one of the grounds is established, the divorce can be granted. It is the intention to separate which carries a test of capacity. A Litigation Guardian or the Public Trustee can make application for a divorce on behalf of a ward provided that one of the three grounds is made out.[54] However, the Litigation Guardian or Public Trustee cannot form the intention to live separate and apart on behalf of the incapacitated person. This is a personal decision that can only be made by the spouse. If the spouse is unable to form the intent to live separate and apart, even if physically this is the case (*e.g.*, where one spouse has been hospitalized), and there has been no cruelty or adultery, then there are no grounds for divorce. A corollary challenge is the capacity for a person to instruct counsel in connection with a divorce.

A divorce operates within estate law to remove a spouse from all entitlements arising from the death of a spouse. If a deceased spouse completed a will while married and was subsequently divorced, the will is read as if the surviving spouse had actually predeceased the testator. A divorced spouse is not entitled to a preferential share. Beneficiary designations, however, such as on a policy of life insurance or RRSP, are unaffected by a divorce.

A divorce does not give rights to claims of equalization, as this is provincial law, governed in Ontario by the *FLA*, and the *DA* states specifically that entitlement under the relevant section is personal between the spouses. Unless a spouse can form the intention to separate, claims arising from the separation, such as equalization, cannot be made by a third party, even a Litigation Guardian or Public Trustee. They can certainly not be made by a person holding a power of attorney.

In contrast, a claim of spousal support can arise from the granting of a divorce and carries no limitation period. It is a minefield

---

[54] *Mordaunt v. Moncreiffe* (1874), L.R. 2 Sc. & Div. 374, 43 L.J.P. & M. 49 (H.L.); *Boswell v. Boswell*, [1951] 2 D.L.R. 847, 1 W.W.R. (N.S.) 629 (Alta. S.C.); *R. v. R.* (1956), 64 Man.R. 161, 19 W.W.R. 155 (Q.B.).

for spouses currently acting as Litigation Guardians, or spouses who seek a placement in a care facility for the incompetent person. By releasing the responsibilities, the spouse may become liable for a payment of spousal support to help maintain the spouse. This provision holds some hope for the family of an incapable person who has entered into what appears to be a predatory marriage. If indeed the incapable person survives long enough for it to become actionable, the new spouse could become liable for spousal support in the event grounds for a divorce can be established, an order for Litigation Guardian can be secured, and a claim for spousal support advanced.

Those in a special relationship with an incapacitated person, such as a spouse acting as a Litigation Guardian, are thus in a difficult position. Only the capable person can form the intention to separate, which places the Litigation Guardian in a position of conflict with his or her ward. The remedy would be to apply to the court to make an appointment for Guardianship, often necessitating the posting of a bond, but not without careful legal analysis of the resulting outcomes.

Effect of the Family Law Act

The *FLA* also has a role to play where capacity is in issue. The *FLA* and its provincial counterparts across Canada are forms of personal rights legislation. This means that the claims available to spouses, parents and children within such statutes may only be exercised by the individual, and cannot be made on his or her behalf, except as authorized by statute.

For example, a person holding a power of attorney cannot effect a separation between the incapacitated person and his or her spouse. This is not a power prescribed by the *Substitute Decisions Act, 1992*[55] ("*SDA*"). Where a spouse is unable to personally form the intention to separate, to instruct counsel, or to act on claims within the *SDA*, a litigation guardian or trustee cannot take up these actions on his or her behalf. The Public Guardian and Trustee or other trustee is limited to seeking an accounting or seeking protection orders of the court.

Because the equalization and support claims within the *FLA* only arise upon the valuation date, a spouse who cannot form the intention to separate, make a claim for improvident depletion or apply for a divorce has no access to his or her statutory entitlements. This limitation in the *FLA* that in effect, only a competent spouse can separate, is profound. It poses tremendous risk to the vulnerable

---

[55] S.O. 1992, c. 30.

spouse irrespective of whether the spouse had capacity at the time of marriage.

There are many instances in which marriages are tragically altered by a catastrophic illness or accident, forcing one spouse into complete dependency and the other into the role of the caregiver. Not all are capable of the transition to caregiver. Sadly, many begin with good intentions, but resentment and entitlement creep in with outcomes that invite intervention of family, friends, the Public Guardian and Trustee and ultimately the courts.

Such intervention is limited. In the case of *Sung Estate*[56] in which the marriage was between an elderly, terminally ill man and his caregiver, lasting a mere number of weeks, Greer J. was satisfied that the grounds had been established for a finding that the marriage was *void ab initio*. What of a marriage on solid ground until a catastrophic event? There is currently no provision either in statute or common law allowing the court to terminate a marriage which has placed an incapacitated individual at unacceptable risk.

Death of the Incapacitated Spouse

Even though marriage automatically revokes a will, the courts have traditionally set the threshold very low for capacity to marry, while those looking to execute a will alone have typically been held to a higher standard of capacity.

The act of marriage immediately and irrevocably invalidates a will. Upon marriage, any will made prior to the marriage, provided that it was not made in contemplation of the marriage, is revoked. Unless a new will is made, the deceased spouse's estate is intestate, treated as if the spouse had never made a will. The relevant section of the *Succession Law Reform Act*[57] ("*SLRA*"), reads:

> 16. A will is revoked by the marriage of the testator except where,
> (a) there is a declaration in the will that it is made in contemplation of the marriage;
> (b) the spouse of the testator elects to take under the will, by an instrument in writing signed by the spouse and filed within one year after the testator's death in the office of the Estate Registrar for Ontario; or

---

[56] (2003), 1 E.T.R. (3d) 296, 37 R.F.L. (5th) 441 *sub nom. Feng v. Sung Estate* (Ont. S.C.J.), affd 11 E.T.R. (3d) 169, 9 R.F.L. (6th) 229 *sub nom. Feng v. Sung Estate* (C.A.).

[57] R.S.O. 1990, c. S.26.

(c) the will is made in exercise of a power of appointment of property which would not in default of the appointment pass to the heir, executor or administrator of the testator or to the persons entitled to the estate of the testator if he or she died intestate.

Under the *SLRA*,

"spouse" means either of two persons who,
    (a) are married to each other, or
    (b) have together entered into a marriage that is voidable or void, in good faith on the part of the person asserting a right under this Act; ("conjoint").

Section 45 of the *SLRA* provides that in the event that a spouse has died without a will, the surviving spouse[58] shall receive the "preferential share" which is the first $200,000 of value within an estate. The remainder is divided in equal shares between the surviving spouse and the deceased's children. Thus, a surviving spouse and her two children would each receive one-third of the remainder. If there are no children, the spouse receives the whole estate.

Children for this purpose are not restricted to dependant children, so that adult children will share the remainder with the surviving spouse. Monies payable to named beneficiaries such as for life insurance and RRSPs (unless the beneficiary was the estate) pass directly to the named beneficiary and do not form part of the estate, and thus are not caught by s. 45 of the *SLRA*.

The only exception to this treatment would be the existence of a court order, such as a prior order for the support of a separated spouse, dependant children, or provisions within a marriage or other domestic contract in which the surviving spouse has released claims against the deceased. Claims that can be released against a spouse within a marriage or other domestic contract include claims of support, dependant's relief, trust claims against property, the preferential share, family law election, or equalization payments.

A discussion follows later with respect to capacity to enter into a marriage or other domestic contract. The threshold for entering into a domestic contract is very high since in entering such a contract one is opting out of statutory entitlements and obligations, while the

---

[58] A married spouse only. The *SLRA* definition of spouse does not include a common-law spouse or a divorced spouse.

capacity to enter into marriage, which gives rise to the entitlements, is currently set very low by the courts.

The practical effect is that adult children who have no right of inheritance or support from their parent's estate (provided the adult child is not incapacitated and a dependant person) will find themselves sharing the remainder of a parent's estate equally with a new step-parent, after that step-parent takes the first $200,000 of net value of the estate.

Predatory marriages are frequently kept secret from the victim's children. In extreme cases, there is no remaining estate on death, as the predatory spouse has seconded the value of the deceased spouse's assets prior to death through influence, gifts, transfer of title or through the use of banking and credit cards.

There is a rarely used and often misunderstood provision within the *FLA* which may afford some relief. Section 7 states that:

Application to court

7. (1) The court may, on the application of a spouse, former spouse or deceased spouse's personal representative, determine any matter respecting the spouses' entitlement under section 5.

Personal action; estates

(2) Entitlement under subsections 5(1), (2) and (3) is personal as between the spouses but,

(a) an application based on subsection 5(1) or (3) and commenced before a spouse's death may be continued by or against the deceased spouse's estate; and

(b) an application based on subsection 5(2) may be made by or against a deceased spouse's estate.

Limitation

(3) An application based on subsection 5(1) or (2) shall not be brought after the earliest of,

(a) two years after the day the marriage is terminated by divorce or judgment of nullity;

(b) six years after the day the spouses separate and there is no reasonable prospect that they will resume cohabitation;

(c) six months after the first spouse's death.

A s. 6 claim under the *FLA* is a claim for equalization that is a payment from the spouse with less family property to the spouse with more net family property. Section 7 allows for the continuance of such a claim if made before death, and also permits a personal representative (executor) to make such a claim against a surviving spouse.

Such applications in practice are rare. They are primarily used to wind up a family court action, or provide a remedy to a surviving spouse who has not been treated equitably within the estate plan or will of the deceased. In the common vernacular, a surviving spouse is entitled to at least as much as he or she would have been had they separated the day before death.

As mentioned above, s. 7 permits a personal representative to make a claim against the surviving spouse. Such a claim is limited to the assets in existence on the date immediately before the date of death. In the event that the net family property of the deceased was lower on the date of death than that of the surviving spouse, then the estate could make a claim for an equalization payment for one-half of the difference. This is rarely the case in the circumstances of a predatory marriage, where the surviving spouse often has considerably less assets than the deceased spouse.

The assets received by the surviving spouse through the preferential share, or through survivorship of joint assets, are not recoverable through the mechanism of s. 6 of the *FLA*, as they are received after the valuation date, that is, after the day before death.

Domestic Contracts

A marriage contract is referred to under the *FLA* as a domestic contract. Domestic contracts also include cohabitation agreements and separation agreements.

Marriage Contract

52. (1) Two persons who are married to each other or intend to marry may enter into an agreement in which they agree on their respective rights and obligations under the marriage or on separation, on the annulment or dissolution of the marriage or on death, including,
   (a) ownership in or division of property;
   (b) support obligations;
   (c) the right to direct the education and moral training of their children, but not the right to custody of or access to their children; and
   (d) any other matter in the settlement of their affairs.

Spouses typically release rights in a domestic contract, such as the right to receive an equalization payment, a preferential share, or an interest in the other's estate. Marriage contracts are strictly construed as they are a manner of "opting out" of the legislative framework. The *FLA* does provide some guidance on the setting aside of a marriage contract:

Setting aside domestic contract

56. (4) A court may, on application, set aside a domestic contract or a provision in it,

    (a) if a party failed to disclose to the other significant assets, or significant debts or other liabilities, existing when the domestic contract was made;

    (b) *if a party did not understand the nature or consequences of the domestic contract*; or

    (c) otherwise in accordance with the law of contract. (emphasis added).

There is much activity in the common law with respect to domestic contracts. It is fair to say that a "boilerplate" contract is not determinative. Parties must do more than fill in the blanks on an Internet form. They must provide full disclosure of the nature and value of all their assets and debts,[59] and understand their entitlements and obligations arising from the marriage in the absence of an agreement. Any lesser standard arguably will entitle either party to set aside an agreement, so that he or she is not bound by the releases or limitation of claims.

Marriage contracts are a serious and expensive affair. They are problematic given the romantic associations of marriage. No first time fiancé wants to be seen as "marrying for money", so many sign ill-advised agreements or fail to seek independent legal advice, to their later regret.

The most common profile for a marriage contract is the second or third marriage. It is far more acceptable for persons with adult children and established family and community ties to prioritize those obligations. Marriage contracts in subsequent marriages allow people to make a limited, agreed and often mutual provision for a spouse, while protecting adult children from the ordinary operation of the law. Many are surprised that no Canadian jurisdiction has enacted a

---

[59] In *LeVan v. LeVan* (2008), 90 O.R. (3d) 1, 51 R.F.L. (6th) 237 (C.A.), leave to appeal to S.C.C. refused [2008] 3 S.C.R. viii, 391 N.R. 391*n*, the Ontario Court of Appeal upheld the trial judge's decision to set aside a marriage contract on the basis that the husband failed to make full disclosure of his significant assets, that his dsiclosure was incomplete and inadequate and that his failure to make full disclosure was a deliberate attempt to mislead his wife.

statutory entitlement for children to inherit from their parents, with the exception of dependant relief.

In some jurisdictions such as Quebec, a marriage contract is a prerequisite to marriage and the practice of entering into one has been normalized. In other jurisdictions there remains a doubting culture. Marriage has the connotation of "good", and that all things will work out, while marriage contracts are often felt to be unpleasant things that invite strife and conflict. It is not widely known that a marriage contract can be entered into at any time before or during a marriage and are useful instruments to protect assets obtained during marriage that would otherwise be subsumed into joint family property. For example, funds from an inheritance applied to a joint mortgage would be lost to the beneficiary spouse unless the spouses entered into a marriage contract that provided for their continued exclusion from net family property, irrespective of their application.

On a threshold basis, a person who lacks the capacity to understand the effect of marriage on prior family obligations will not appreciate the need to enter into a marriage contract. Should the need for a marriage contract be pressed by others, the marriage contract can be later set aside in the event that it was not clear whether the spouse fully understood the nature or consequences of the domestic contract.

Nonetheless, there remains one way in which an incapacitated person can enter into an enforceable domestic contract, such as a marriage contract. Section 55(3) of the *FLA* provides that:

Guardian of property
55. (3) If a mentally incapable person has a guardian of property other than his or her own spouse, the guardian may enter into a domestic contract or give any waiver or consent under this Act on the person's behalf, subject to the approval of the court, given in advance.

P.G.T.
55. (4) In all other cases of mental incapacity, the Public Guardian and Trustee has power to act on the person's behalf in accordance with subsection (3).

The requirement that the court approve the domestic contract in advance is absolute, as tested in *Parker v. Atkinson*.[60] The daughter appointed to act as guardian of her father's financial affairs sought to uphold a marriage contract entered into by herself as committee of her

---

[60] (1993), 104 D.L.R. (4th) 279, 48 R.F.L. (3d) 193 (Ont. U.F.C.).

father's affairs and her father's second spouse. The father had died and the spouse had become incompetent by the time of the hearing. The spouse was represented by the Public Trustee. The court refused to cure the marriage contract for its failure to have had prior court approval, a requirement likely unknown to the daughter. The contract was thus voided, allowing for assets to pass to the spouse, even though the spouse had been competent and properly advised at the time of signing the marriage contract.

In summary, the nature and effect of marriage and other domestic contracts which govern the rights arising from marriage are seen by the legislators and the courts to be of great importance. One cannot contract out of such rights without complying with the formalities of the *FLA*. Mentally incapable persons can only rely upon domestic contracts prepared by their guardian or trust if prior court approval has been obtained.

This chapter has reviewed the basic requirements of capacity to marry, good faith, forced marriage, capacity to separate, death of an incapacitated spouse, marriage contracts, and the capacity to divorce. We can now delve into the treatment of capacity to marry in the case law in the next chapter.

CHAPTER 6

CASE LAW REVIEW

In the preceding chapters, we have looked at demographics, marriage, testamentary freedom and the requirements for capacity to marry. We have set out various concepts that are integral to understanding capacity to marry, especially in the context of predatory marriages, which is the central theme of this book. This chapter features a review of both historical and current case law on the topic of capacity to marry. The recent treatment of capacity to marry by the courts is the inspiration for our investigation and an area in which further development is possible and arguably desirable.

Predatory Marriages

The focus of this book is on incapacity and marriage. The concerns raised reflect the changing dynamics of our society. Not a new, but rather a developing phenomenon, is marriage of a predatory nature. These are marriages entered into for the singular purpose of exploitation, personal gain or profit by unprincipled individuals who are taking advantage of the vulnerable, dependant, elderly, cognitively impaired, and incapable.

The growing number of disputes concerning testamentary planning, wills, planning for incapacity, including the granting and use of power of attorney documents, and of guardianship, are indicative of the consequences and turmoil associated with the increasing complexity of family structures, the increase in accumulated wealth, as well as increased longevity. Given the significant aging population within Canada, attention must be paid by lawmakers, among others, to the nexus between aging, reduced decisional capacity, and abuse.

The continuing need for civility and for societal protections must be balanced against the preservation of autonomy, human rights, freedoms, and independence. This need is never static. Protection of the vulnerable must be balanced against an excess of societal control. There presently exist certain laws to protect the vulnerable, the dependant and the victimized. Our societal values also remain fluid. The development of accepted societal norms can result from advocacy, or sometimes from crisis.

The statistics confirm that our population is aging rapidly. With longevity comes an increase in the occurrence of medical ailments such as dementia in varying types and degrees, as well as delirium, delusional disorders, Alzheimer's, cognitive disorders and other conditions involving reduced functioning and capability. There are a wide variety of mental disorders that affect capacity and increase an individual's vulnerability and dependence. Other factors affecting capacity include, *inter alia*, normal aging, disorders such as depression which are often untreated or undiagnosed, schizophrenia, bipolar disorder, psychotic disorders, delusions, debilitating illnesses, senility, drug and alcohol abuse, and addiction.

In our experience, civil marriages are solemnized with increasing frequency under circumstances where one party to the marriage is incapable of understanding, appreciating, and of formulating a choice, to marry. Unscrupulous opportunists too often get away with taking advantage of those with diminished reasoning ability purely for financial profit.

One circumstance of particular concern arises where one individual may marry another in order to gain some advantage. We have already referred to this situation in preceding chapters with the term 'predatory marriages'. This is not a term that is in common use. However, it does effectively capture the situations of concern in which one person marries another of limited capacity with the object of personal gain. Given that marriage brings with it a wide range of entitlements, there are those who may marry primarily in pursuit of these advantages. A marriage may be referred to as 'predatory' where one party seeks such advantages *and* the other party is unable to appreciate this possibility or its consequences. In many cases, the attendant consequences may be future consequences to the person him or herself, or may be consequences for his or her children or grandchildren, who would otherwise have been provided for by this individual.

So-called predatory marriages are often accompanied by aliena-tion from the marital subject's family. That is, the person who seeks the marriage for his or her own gain often either takes advantage of an existing situation, or takes pains to create a situation where the subject is distanced from all of his or her other friends or family. There is often a period prior to the marriage during which the family of the incapable person is deliberately and purposefully alienated by his or her soon-to-be spouse. In other words, active steps are taken to prevent, prohibit, discourage and avoid contact with others who may care for the person. It is this distance from friends and family that is referred to as 'alienation' and that facilitates a situation in which the subject agrees to turn all of his or her assets over to the new spouse at the expense of the usual beneficiaries: namely, the individual's children and grand-children. Under such circumstances, family and friends often have no knowledge of the marriage until well after the fact.

While the concept of alienation is not overtly referred to in the case law concerning the capacity to marry, it is a concept that appears frequently in the context of family law cases. There is in fact a considerable body of psychological literature devoted to the topic. In the family law context, the concept of "parental alienation syndrome" ("PAS") has become a recurring, although controversial, theme. That is, there is still a great deal of confusion about the nature and dimensions of PAS.[1] Many question whether the identification of the so-called syndrome is based on any reliable research or data. PAS is said to occur where a child belittles one parent and in some cases wants nothing to do with him or her and the cause of this state of affairs is identified as the active intervention to this end by the other parent. Something similar to the PAS can be thought to occur as a precursor to a predatory marriage. That is, instead of one parent turning a child against the other parent, here the soon-to-be spouse turns a vulnerable individual against his or her existing family and friends, convincing the person that no one else cares about him or her.

Capacity to Marry in Historical Case Law

Of course, an individual is free to choose a spouse over his or her other family or friends so long as he or she is capable of making such a choice. This section will discuss the historical development of the concept of capacity to marry.

In *McElroy(Re)*[2] the court had the following to say about the test for capacity to marry:

> In order to determine that a person had the capacity to marry, the Court must ascertain that he was capable of understanding the nature of

---

[1]   D.C. Rand, "The Spectrum of Parental Alienation Syndrome" (1997), 15 Am. J. Forensic Psych. No. 3.

[2]   (1979), 93 D.L.R. (3d) 522, 22 O.R. (2d) 381 (Surr. Ct.).

the marriage contract, free from the influence of morbid delusions on the subject of marriage. The onus of showing lack of capacity is on those who attack the validity of marriage.

Where a person appreciates the duties and responsibilities which marriage creates before and at the time of the marriage, understands the marriage contract he is about to enter into, and has no mental illness or defect, the marriage is valid.[3]

In this case, the court was not convinced that there was incapacity to marry. In arriving at this determination, the court set out a test referring to the "duties and responsibilities" which must be appreciated before and at the time of marriage in order for there to be the requisite capacity. In other words, the test defined by the court did not focus on the legal implications of marriage, but instead the duties and responsibilities associated with the union.

On the other side of the equation, consent can be vitiated by oppression or duress: In *S. (A.) v. S. (A.)*[4] the court observed as follows: "To constitute duress, it must be established that the applicant's mind was so overcome by oppression that there was an absence of free choice".[5]

The requirements for a valid marriage that therefore emerge from the case law are as follows:

1. the marriage must be voluntary;[6]
2. the marriage must be consummated;[7]
3. there must be an absence of a prior existing marriage;[8]
4. there must be consent;[9]

---

[3] *Supra*, at p. 523 (D.L.R.).

[4] (1988), 65 O.R. (2d) 720, 15 R.F.L. (3d) 443 (U.F.C.).

[5] *Supra*, at p. 734 (O.R.).

[6] *Hendricks v. Canada (Procureur General)* (2004), 238 D.L.R. (4th) 577, [2004] R.J.Q. 851 (C.A.).

[7] *Davison v. Sweeney* (2005), 255 D.L.R. (4th) 757, [2005] 9 W.W.R. 698 (B.C.S.C.); *Shaw v. Shaw*, [1946] 1 D.L.R. 168, [1945] 3 W.W.R. 577 (B.C.C.A); *Heil v. Heil*, [1942] 1 D.L.R. 657, [1942] S.C.R. 160; *Gajamugan v. Gajamugan* (1979), 10 R.F.L. (2d) 280, [1979] O.J. No. 39 (QL) (H.C.J.); *De Reneville v. De Reneville*, [1947] P. 168, [1948] 1 All E.R. 560; *C. (H.L.) v. L. (M.A.)* (2003), 45 R.F.L. (5th) 106, 125 A.C.W.S. (3d) 460 (B.C.S.C.).

[8] *Savelieff v. Glouchkoff* (1964), 45 D.L.R. (2d) 520, 48 W.W.R. 335 (B.C.C.A.).

[9] *Durham v. Durham* (1885), 10 P.D. 80, at p. 82; *Hunter v. Edney* (1881), 10 P.D. 93, at pp. 95-6; *Reynolds v. Reynolds*, [1966] 58 W.W.R. 87, [1966] B.C.J. No. 21 (QL) (S.C.); *S. (A.) v. S. (A.)*, *supra*, footnote 4; *Kerr v. Kerr*, [1952] 4 D.L.R. 578, 60 Man. R. 118 (C.A.).

5. the participants must not be intoxicated[10] or under the influence of drugs;[11] and
6. the marriage must not be induced by duress or coercion.[12]

Even 'artifices' and 'misrepresentations' will not necessarily operate to vitiate consent. For example, in *Sullivan v. Sullivan*,[13] the court found that even the most extreme scheming and deception used to 'induce' marriage will not nullify it where consent was freely given:

> I say the strongest case you could establish of the most deliberate plot leading to a marriage the most unseemly in all disproportions of rank, of fortune, of habits of life, and even of age itself, would not enable this Court to release him from chains which, though forged by others, he had riveted on himself. If he is capable of consent, and has consented, the law does not ask how the consent has been induced. His own consent, however procured, is his own act . . . . The law looks no further back.[14]

However, fraud or duress will operate to vitiate consent to marry. In *Scott v. Sebright*,[15] the court, in a petition to seek a declaration of a nullity of a marriage which was granted, stated that:

> The Courts of law have always refused to recognize as binding contracts to which the consent of either party has been obtained by fraud or duress, and the validity of a contract of marriage must be tested and determined in precisely the same manner as that of any other contract. True it is that in contracts of marriage there is an interest involved above and beyond that of the immediate parties. Public policy requires that marriages should not be lightly set aside, and there is in some cases the strongest temptation to the parties more immediately interested to act in collusion in obtaining a dissolution of the marriage tie. These reasons necessitate great care and circumspection on the part of the tribunal, but they in no wise alter the principle or the grounds on which this, like any other contract, may be avoided. . . . The difficulty consists not in any uncertainty of the law on the subject, but in its application to the facts of each individual case.[16]

---

[10] *Roblin v. Roblin* (1881), 28 Gr. 439 (Ont. Ch.); *Ward v. Ward* (1985), 66 N.B.R. (2d) 44, [1985] N.B.J. No. 296 (QL) (Q.B.).

[11] *Meilen v. Andersson* (1977), 6 A.R. 427, [1977] 2 A.C.W.S. 283 (S.C. (T.D.)).

[12] *Scott v. Sebright* (1886), 12 P.D. 21 at pp. 21, 24, [1886-90] All E.R. Rep. 363; *S. (A.) v. S. (A.)* (1988), 65 O.R. (2d) 720 at p. 734, 15 R.F.L. (3d) 443 (U.F.C.).

[13] (1818), 161 E.R. 728, [1818] 2 Hag. Con. 238, affd 3 Phillim 45 *sub nom. Sullivan v. Oldacre.*

[14] *Supra*, at para. 248.

[15] *Supra*, footnote 12.

[16] *Supra*, footote 12, at pp. 23-4.

What follows is a discussion of the concept of marriage that arises from a review of historical case law. As will be illustrated, the concept of marriage is not consistently understood and as a result, the test for capacity to enter into a marriage is fluid, varying greatly on the particular circumstances of the facts before the court.

(1) Marriage as Civil Contract

One line of old English cases that address capacity to marry emphasizes the equivalency between the capacity to marry and the capacity to enter into any civil contract. A series of cases discussed below all address the issue of whether at the time of the marriage, the respondent was of sound mind and so capable of entering into a contract. These cases treat the contract of marriage as a simple subset of civil contract law in general.

In *Lacey v. Lacey*[17] the essence of the marriage contract was described as follows:

> Thus at law, the essence of a marriage contract is an engagement between a man and a woman to live together and to love one another as husband and wife to the exclusion of all others. It is a simple contract which does not require high intelligence to comprehend. It does not involve consideration of a large variety of circumstances required in other acts involving others, such as in the making of a Will. In addition, the character of consent for this particular marriage did not involve consideration of other circumstances normally required by other persons contemplating marriage — such as establishing a source of income, maintaining a home, or contemplation of children. Were the parties then capable of understanding the nature of the contract they were entering into?[18]

In that case, the court found that John and Margaret Lacey, who were of an advanced age, were lonely, seeking companionship and had quite limited expectations of their marriage. The court did not however, set the marriage aside on this basis in reliance upon the concept of marriage as a simple contract.

In *Durham v. Durham*[19] the court again had to determine whether the respondent was capable of understanding the nature of the marriage contract and the duties and responsibilities that it creates. There was also a question as to whether the respondent was free from

---

[17] [1983] B.C.J. No. 1016 (QL) (S.C.).

[18] *Supra*, at para. 31.

[19] (1885), 10 P.D. 80 [hereinafter *Durham*].

the influence of morbid delusions upon the subject of marriage. The petition by the Right Honourable the Earl of Durham was for a declaration of nullity of his marriage to Ethel Elizabeth Louisa, Countess of Durham by reason that at the time of the celebration of the marriage, she was of unsound mind. The court ultimately concluded that under the circumstances of the case, the burden of proof had not been discharged and the marriage was upheld. In contemplating the issue before the court, Sir J. Hannen, President, made the following more general remarks about the contract of marriage and the requisite level of capacity required to enter into it:

> I may say this much in the outset, that it appears to me that the contract of marriage is a very simple one, which does not require a high degree of intelligence to comprehend.
>
> It is an engagement between a man and a woman to live together, and love one another as husband and wife, to the exclusion of all others. This is expanded in the promises of the marriage ceremony by words having reference to the natural relations which spring from that engagement, such as protection on the part of the man, and submission on the part of the woman. I agree with the Solicitor General, that a mere comprehension of the words of the promises exchanged is not sufficient. The mind of one of the parties may be capable of understanding the language used, but may yet be affected by such delusions, or other symptoms of insanity, as may satisfy the tribunal that there was not a real appreciation of the engagement apparently entered into. It seems to me that the determination of the case must depend upon whether I come to the conclusion that there were such symptoms of insanity manifested by the respondent on the 28th of October, 1882 . . .. I am bound to take into consideration the fact that she has now become manifestly insane. I must look at the nature of that insanity, and form an opinion from the general history of the case, whether it is recent or sudden in its inception, or whether it has been of slow growth, and whether it had begun before the marriage and had by that time reached a stage which incapacitated the respondent from entering into the contract of marriage.[20]

In *Cannon v. Smalley*[21] there was a petition by a husband for a nullity of marriage by reason of the insanity of the respondent at the time of the marriage. In this case, the court did not declare the marriage a nullity since there was no evidence to sustain the proposition that the respondent was incapable. The evidence did not establish the timing of incapacity.

---

[20] *Supra*, at p. 82.
[21] (1885), 10 P.D. 96.

At issue in *Estate of Park (Re)*,[22] was the question of whether the deceased had capacity to marry. Justice Singleton articulated the test for the validity of marriage in that case as follows:

> In considering whether or not a marriage is invalid on the ground that one of the parties was of unsound mind at the time it was celebrated the test to be applied is whether he or she was capable of understanding the nature of the contract into which he or she was entering, free from the influence of morbid delusions on the subject. To ascertain the nature of the contract of marriage a person must be mentally capable of appreciating that it involves the duties and responsibilities normally attaching to marriage.[23]

Justice Birkett added to this the following remarks on the subject:

> The contract of marriage in its essence is one of simplicity. There can be degrees of capacity apart from soundness of mind. It is understandable that an illiterate man, perfectly sound of mind, but not of high quality, might be able to understand the contract of marriage in its simplicity, but who, coming into a sudden accession of wealth, might be quite incapable of making anything in the nature of a complicated will, but degrees of unsoundness of mind cannot have much relevance to the question whether it is shown that a person was not mentally capable of understanding the contract into which he or she had entered.[24]

In the same decision, Hodson L.J. added dicta to clarify the question of whether consent to marriage required a lesser degree of soundness of mind than did the capacity to make a will. Though affirming the decision of Karminsky J., Hodson L.J.'s view was that, ". . . there is no sliding scale of soundness of mind by reference to which different matters on which the law is required to take cognisance may be measured".[25] On this point, at trial, Karminski J. differed, stating that in his opinion, there is "a lesser degree of capacity is required to consent to a marriage than in the making of a will".[26]

The test for a valid marriage set out in that case by Karminski J. was as follows: "i. the parties must understand the nature of the

---

[22] [1954] P. 112, [1953] 2 All E.R. 1411, affg [1954] P. 89, [1953] 2 All E.R. Rep. [hereinafter *Park*].

[23] *Supra*, at p. 1411 (C.A.) (headnote).

[24] *Supra*, at p. 1411 (C.A.) (headnote).

[25] *Supra*, at p. 1435 (C.A.) (All E.R.)

[26] *Supra*, at p. 413 (P.D.) (All E.R.).

marriage contract; ii. the parties must understand the rights and responsibilities which marriage entails; iii. each party must be able to take care of his or her person and property; iv. it is not enough that the party appreciates that he is taking part in a marriage ceremony or that he should be able merely to follow the words of the ceremony; if he lacks that which is involved under heads (i), (ii) and (iii) the marriage is invalid. . . . The question for consideration is whether he sanely comprehended the nature of the marriage contract". Ultimately, the court recognized the difficulty in formulating the right test for capacity to marry, but held that the requisite capacity to marry was effectively equivalent to the capacity to enter into any binding contract.[27]

This equivalency between capacity to contract and to marry was reiterated in *Turner v. Meyers*.[28] In that case, a man successfully brought an action to set aside his own marriage on the grounds that he himself was incapable:

> [T]hat a defect of incapacity invalidates the contract of marriage, as well as any other contract . . . that a marriage of an insane person could not be invalidated on that account, founded, I presume, on some notion that prevailed in the dark ages, of the mysterious nature of a contract of marriage, in which its spiritual nature almost entirely obliterated its civil character. In modern times, it has been considered, in its proper light, as a civil contract, as well as a religious vow, and, like all civil contracts, will be invalidated by want of consent of capable persons.[29]

In *Browning v. Reane*[30] the deceased, Mary Reane, was 70 years old and the man she married only 40. At issue was the deceased's capacity to enter into a legally binding contract of marriage. The court determined that the marriage was in law invalid by virtue of the fact that the deceased was incapable of entering into the marriage. In arriving at this conclusion, the court remarked upon the most common causes of incapacity to marry, namely 'mental weakness' and 'imbecility':

> "A fourth incapacity is, want of reason; without a competent share of which, as no others, so neither can the matrimonial contract be valid. It was formerly adjudged that the issue of an ideot was

---

[27] *Supra*, at p. 1417 (C.A.) (All E.R.), affg *Park v. Park*, [1953] 2 All E.R. 408, [1954] P. 89 (P.D.).

[28] (1808), 161 E.R. 600, 1 Haig. Con. 414.

[29] *Supra*, at p. 601 (E.R.).

[30] (1812), 161 E.R. 1080, [1803-13] All E.R. Rep. 265 [hereinafter *Browning*].

legitimate, and, consequently, that his marriage was valid. A strange determination! since consent is absolutely requisite to matrimony; and neither ideots, nor lunatics, are capable of consenting to anything; and, therefore, the civil law judged much more sensibly, when it made such deprivations of reason a previous impediment, though not a cause of divorce if they happened after marriage. And modern resolutions have adhered to the reason of the civil law, by determining that the marriage of a lunatic, not be in a lucid interval, was absolutely void." [Mr. Justice Blackstone]

Here, then, the law, and the good sense of the law, are clearly laid down; want of reason must, of course, invalidate a contract, and the most important contract of life, the very essence of which is consent. It is not material whether the want of consent arises from ideotcy or lunacy, or from both combined, nor does it seem necessary, in this case, to enter into any disquisition of what is ideotcy, and what is lunacy. Complete ideotcy, total fatuity from the birth, rarely occurs; a much more common case is mental weakness and imbecillity, increased as a person grows up and advances in age from various supervening causes, so as to produce unsoundness of mind. Objects of this sort have occurred to the observation of most people. If the incapacity be such, arising from either or both causes, that the party is incapable of understanding the nature of the contract itself, and incapable from mental imbecillity to take care of his or her own person and property, such an individual cannot dispose of her person and property by the matrimonial contract, any more than by any other contract. The exact line of separation between reason and incapacity may be difficult to be found and marked out in the abstract; though it may not be difficult, in most cases, to decide upon the result of the circumstances; and this appears to be a case of that description, the circumstances being such as to leave no doubt upon my mind.[31]

(2) Distinct Nature of Marriage

A parallel line of cases emphasizes not the equivalency between the capacity to marry and to enter into any other civil contract, but rather the distinct nature of marriage. That is, the focus in these cases is on an appreciation of the particular duties and responsibilities that attach to marriage.

In *Durham*,[32] the court decided the matter upon the particular facts of the case but also established that the issue properly defined was as follows: "whether or not the individual had capacity to

---

[31] *Supra*, at p. 1081 (E.R.).
[32] (1885), 10 P.D. 80.

understand the nature of the contract, and the duties and responsibilities which it creates?" There were no precise legal criteria upon which to establish the answer to this question. The court in *Jackson v. Jackson*[33] as well as in *Forster v. Forster*[34] employed a similar test, namely, "whether the respondent was capable of understanding the nature of the contract he was entering into, free from the influence of morbid delusions on the subject".[35]

In *Spier (Re)*,[36] Willmer J. clarified the specific capacity required for marriage, again emphasizing the need to understand the nature of the specific contract and the duties and responsibilities of marriage:

> [I]t was not sufficient merely to be able to understand the words of the ceremony or even to know that the party was going through a ceremony. There must be capacity to understand the nature of the contract and the duties and responsibilities which it created, and from *Browning v. Reane* ... there must also be a capacity to take care of his or her own person and property .... But as pointed out in *Durham, supra*, marriage was a very simple contract which did not require a high degree of intelligence to contract; certainly it did not call for so high a degree of mental capacity as the making of a will.[37]

In that case, the court pronounced against the will and declared the marriage to be invalid.

(3) Simplicity of Marriage

Historical case law on the question of capacity to marry differs in terms of the emphasis placed on marriage as a contract like any other, as opposed to a contract of a highly distinct kind with particular duties and responsibilities.

There does, however, seem to be general consensus in the historical case law that the contract of marriage is a simple one and that capacity to marry should be evaluated on this basis.

In *Park*, the court stated that a marriage is in its essence a simple contract which any person of either sex of normal intelligence should readily be able to comprehend.[38] Similar language is found in *Hunter*

---

[33]   [1908] 1 P. 308.

[34]   [1923] 39 T.L.R. 658, at pp. 658-59.

[35]   *Supra*, footnote 33.

[36]   [1947] W.N. 46 (P.D.) [Hereinafter *Spier*].

[37]   *Supra*, at p. 46.

[38]   [1954] P. 112, [1953] 2 All E.R. 1411, affg [1954] P. 89, [1953] 2 All E.R. Rep. [hereinafter *Park*].

v. Edney, wherein it was stated that, "no high intellectual standard is required in consenting to a marriage".[39]

The authors contend that the degree of mental capacity to contract marriage is not less, the contract is not simple, and the standard to be attributed is arguably as high as the standard required for the capacity to make a will, for testamentary capacity or for the capacity to manage property.

(4)   Companion Capacity to Manage Property

In tension with the concept of marriage as a simple contract is the idea expressed in a number of cases that a person must also have the capacity to manage his or her own property in order to be capable of marriage. See, for example, *Browning*[40] and *Spier*.[41]

As a result of this requisite capacity to manage property, in *Spier* the court determined that the deceased testator lacked both testamentary capacity and the capacity to enter into a marriage. Dicta in that case suggest that incapacity to manage property may in itself be sufficient to give rise to a finding of lack of capacity to marry.

Browning also refers to both capacity to manage one's person and property as prerequisites for capacity to marry.

In what we have seen above, it is clear that there is no single definition of marriage, or the capacity to enter into it, that is common to all the cases that treat the topic. The concept of marriage varies from that of a 'simple' contract, requiring very little to understand such that the threshold of understanding the rights and responsibilities of marriage is low, to a far more stringent requirement that capacity to manage one's person personal and property matters is a prerequisite for the capacity to marry.

In the section that follows, recent treatment of marriage and capacity to marry in the case law is discussed.

Capacity to Marry in Current Case Law

The focus of this section is on the Ontario cases of *Banton v. Banton*[42] and *Sung Estate (Re)*[43] as well as a review of the 1994 British

---

[39]   (1881), 10 P.D. 93, at pp. 95-96.

[40]   (1812), 161 E.R. 1080, 2 Phill. Ecc. 69.

[41]   *Supra*, footnote 36.

[42]   (1998), 164 D.L.R. (4th) 176, 66 O.T.C. 161 (Gen. Div.), supp. reasons 164 D.L.R. (4th) at p. 244, 83 A.C.W.S. (3d) 531 (Gen. Div.) [hereinafter *Banton*].

[43]   (2003), 1 E.T.R. (3d) 296, 37 R.F.L. (5th) 441 *sub nom. Feng v. Sung Estate*

Columbia Supreme Court case of *Hart v. Cooper*[44] and the 2000 case from Alberta, namely, *Barrett Estate v. Dexter*.[45]

These cases all share certain unifying features. They involve elderly individuals in need of companionship or care-giving who ultimately marry the individuals who provide for these needs. The marriage usually occurs without the involvement of other family or friends after a period of alienation from these individuals.

The facts of *Hart* are as follows: Mr. Smiglicki, 76, and Ms. Hart 58, were married by way of a civil marriage ceremony. Before the marriage, Mr. Smiglicki learned that he had a terminal illness with little more than a month to live. More than six years earlier, Mr. Smiglicki had made out a will naming his three children as the beneficiaries. This will was revoked upon his marriage to Ms. Hart. The children challenged the validity of the marriage on the grounds of Smiglicki's mental incapacity to enter into the contract of marriage. The children also alleged that Ms. Hart had alienated Mr. Smiglicki from his family.

In terms of standing, *Hart* confirms that anyone with a financial interest as a result of a marriage can make a claim against its validity.

The test for capacity to marry articulated by the court was as follows:

> A person is mentally capable of entering into a marriage contract only if he/she has the capacity to understand the nature of the contract and the duties and responsibilities it creates. The recognition that a ceremony of marriage is being performed or the mere comprehension of the words employed and the promises exchanged is not enough if, because of the state of mind, there is no real appreciation of the engagement entered into; *Durham v. Durham; Hunter v. Edney* (otherwise *Hunter*); *Cannon v. Smalley* (otherwise *Cannon*) (1885), L.R. 10 P.D. 80 at 82 and 95. But the contract is a very simple one — not at all difficult to understand. The wording of the ceremony performed between Mr. Smiglicki and Ms. Hart pursuant to the *Marriage Act*, R.S.B.C. 1979, c. 251 described it only as "a voluntary union of one man to one woman to the exclusion of all others".[46]

(Ont. S.C.J.), affd 11 E.T.R. (3d) 169, 9 R.F.L. (6th) 229 *sub nom. Feng v. Sung Estate* (C.A.) [hereinafter *Sung Estate*].

[44] (1994), 2 E.T.R. (2d) 168, 45 A.C.W.S. (3d) 284 (B.C.S.C.) [hereinafter *Hart*].

[45] (2000), 34 E.T.R. (2d) 1, 268 A.R. 101 (Q.B.) [hereinafter *Barrett Estate*].

[46] *Hart, supra*, footnote 44, at para. 30.

Note here that the court emphasizes the simplicity of the marriage contract, embracing the test that relies on the concept of marriage as a 'simple contract' and eschewing the more involved standard of capacity to manage one's person and property.

The court then proceeded to describe the appropriate burden of proof as follows:

> Where, as here, a marriage has, in form, been properly celebrated, the burden of proving a lack of mental capacity is born by the party who challenges the validity. What is required is proof of a preponderance of evidence. The evidence must be of a sufficiently clear and definite character as to constitute more than a "mere" preponderance as is required in ordinary civil cases: *Reynolds v. Reynolds* (1966), 58 W.W.R. 87 at 90-91 (B.C.S.C.) quoting from *Kerr v. Kerr* (1952), 5 W.W.R. (N.S.) 385 (Man. C.A.).[47]

The court in this case did not accept the medical evidence of Mr. Smiglicki's incapacity and concluded that the burden of proof borne by the three children had not been discharged. The court added that there was no evidence given to suggest that Ms. Hart ever profited financially from either her marriage to Mr. Smiglicki or from her marriage to her previous husbands. Additionally, the court found that Ms. Hart's motivation in marrying Mr. Smiglicki was not otherwise relevant to the determination of his mental state at the time of the marriage ceremony. Accordingly, the marriage was upheld as valid, and the will previously executed remained revoked.

It is difficult to determine from the reasons in this case whether and to what extent the court considered the allegations of alienation and potentially predatory circumstances that the family asserted preceded the marriage.

In contrast, in the case of *Barrett Estate* the court declared the marriage performed between Arlene Dexter-Barrett and Dwight Wesley Barrett to be a nullity, based upon a finding that Mr. Barrett lacked the legal capacity to enter into any form of marriage contract.

Mr. Dwight Barrett was a 93-year-old widower, who made the acquaintance of Arlene Dexter Barrett in a senior's club. Ms. Barrett was 54 years of age. Ms. Barrett rented a room in Mr. Barrett's house, an arrangement facilitated by Mr. Barrett's son and an attorney. A rental agreement was entered into. The three children of Mr. Barrett became suspicious of the increasing influence that Ms. Dexter was

---

[47] *Hart, supra*, footnote 44, at para. 31.

exerting on their father. A further agreement was executed, giving Ms. Dexter the privilege of living in Mr. Barrett's home during his lifetime, and for one year thereafter. Shortly after this agreement was entered into, Ms. Dexter and Mr. Barrett obtained a marriage licence. Ms. Dexter made an appointment with the marriage commissioner, and her daughter and son-in-law attended as witnesses. The marriage was not performed as apparently the son-in-law had a change of heart about acting as a witness. Ms. Dexter then made another appointment with a different marriage commissioner. On this occasion, the limousine driver and additional taxi cab driver acted as witnesses. Mr. Barrett advised his granddaughter of the marriage when she came to visit him on the day after the wedding.

Mr. Barrett then proceeded to draft a new will, appointing his new wife as executor, and gifting to her the house and furniture as well as the residue of his estate. A capacity assessment was conducted shortly thereafter. Mr. Barrett's son brought an application to declare the marriage a nullity on the basis of lack of mental capacity to marry, or alternatively, that Mr. Barrett was unduly influenced by Ms. Dexter such that he was not acting of his own will and accord.

There was evidence that at the time of the marriage, Mr. Barrett told the marriage commissioner that he believed that the marriage was necessary in order for him to avoid placement in a nursing home. The evidence of alienation included the removal of family pictures from his home, interference with planned family gatherings, Ms. Dexter speaking for Mr. Barrett and advising him against answering his son's reasonable questions, as well as evidence that Ms. Dexter was writing documents on Mr. Barrett's behalf.

The assessing doctors were unanimous in finding that Mr. Barrett lacked the capacity to marry. Their findings included that Mr. Barrett had significant deficiencies which prevented him from effectively considering the consequences of his marriage on his family and estate. They also found that Mr. Barrett was vulnerable to influence prior to the marriage and that Ms. Dexter's actions were consistent with the alienation of Mr. Barrett from his family.

On the issue of capacity to marry, one of the doctors, Dr. Malloy, significantly expressed the opinion that a person must understand the nature of the marriage contract, the state of previous marriages, as well as the affect that the marriage may have on one's children. Dr. Malloy testified that it is possible for an assessor or the court to set a high or low threshold for this measurement, but that in his opinion, "no matter where you set the threshold, Dwight [Mr. Baxter] failed".[48]

In considering the evidence before it, the court employed the following test for capacity to marry from *Durham*: "A capacity to understand the nature of the contract and the duties and responsibilities which it creates".[49] The onus of proof was on the parties attacking the marriage. Because of the strength of the medical evidence and the relative weakness of the lay witnesses' evidence, Wilkins J. held that the plaintiff had proven that Mr. Baxter lacked the requisite capacity to marry on a balance of probabilities and declared the marriage null and void. Accordingly, the court found it unnecessary to decide the issue of undue influence. The expert's characterization here of the capacity to marry and the standard to be employed is progressive. It is very close to the standard ultimately endorsed by the authors of this book.

In the case of *Banton*,[50] a number of issues were brought before the court by George Banton's children, including whether Mr. Banton had capacity to make wills in 1994, and 1995, whether the wills were procured by undue influence, and whether Mr. Banton had capacity to enter into the marriage with Muna Yassin.

Justice Cullity's decision in this case includes an extensive examination of the central facts and issues.

The facts of the case were as follows. Mr. Banton made a will when he was 84 years old, distributing his property equally amongst his five children. Shortly thereafter, he moved into a retirement home. Within a year of moving into a retirement home, he met Muna Yassin, a 31-year-old waitress working in the home's restaurant. At this time, Mr. Banton was terminally ill with prostate cancer. He was also by all accounts, depressed. In addition, he was in a weakened physical state requiring a walker and was incontinent. In 1994, at 88 years of age, Mr. Banton married Muna Yassin at her apartment. Two days after the marriage, he and Ms. Yassin met with a solicitor who was instructed to prepare a power of attorney in favour of Ms. Yassin, as well as a will leaving all of Mr. Banton's property to her. Identical planning documents were later prepared after an assessment of Mr. Banton's capacity to manage his property and to grant a power of attorney. Shortly after the new identical documents were prepared in 1995, a further capacity assessment was performed, which found Mr.

---

[48] *Barrett, supra,* footnote 45, at para. 72.
[49] (1885), 10 P.D. 80, at p. 82.
[50] *Supra,* footnote 42, at p. 244 (D.L.R.).

Banton incapable of managing property, but capable with respect to personal care. Mr. Banton died in 1996.

Justice Cullity found that George Banton lacked testamentary capacity to make the wills in 1994, and 1995, and that the wills were obtained through the exertion of undue influence. In spite of these findings and in spite of the fact that the marriage to Ms. Yassin revoked all existing wills, Cullity J. held that Mr. Banton did have the capacity to enter into the marriage. Justice Cullity reviewed the law on the validity of marriages, emphasizing the disparity in the tests for testamentary capacity, capacity to manage property, capacity to give a Power of Attorney for Property, capacity to give a Power of Attorney for Personal Care and capacity to marry:

> With the possible exception of the law relating to capacity to marry, the applicable legal principles are reasonably settled. As in other cases involving elderly testators, the difficulty lies in finding the facts and applying the principles to them. The difficulty is accentuated in this case by the existence of different legal tests for determining capacity to marry; testamentary capacity; capacity to manage property; capacity to give a power of attorney for property; capacity to give a power of attorney for personal care. Each of these is relevant in varying degrees to the issues in this case. It is clear that capacity or incapacity for one such purpose does not necessarily determine the question for other purposes. Although in each case the question may depend, at least, in part, upon the individual's cognitive powers, the nature of understanding required is not the same. The tests are, therefore, different, and this is now made explicit in the provisions of the *Substitute Decisions Act*, dealing with capacity to manage property, capacity to give a power of attorney with respect to property, capacity for personal care, and capacity to give a power of attorney for personal care.[51]

Justice Cullity's review of the case law and observation that the legal principles relating to capacity to marry are not settled accords with our view in light of the review of case law above.

Justice Cullity explores the idea of marriage as a legal contract, but distinguishes the marital contract on the basis of the applicable presumptions respecting undue influence:

> Marriage is, of course, a legal contract, and to some extent, it is governed by the laws applicable to contracts in general. I am satisfied, however, that it is not subject to the operation or application of the presumptions and principles which determine whether contracts may be

---

[51] *Supra*, footnote 42, at p. 189 (D.L.R.).

avoided on the grounds of undue influence. Fraud, of course, is another matter, but the evidence in this case does not support such a finding. To that extent, authority such as *Portsmouth (Countess) v. Portsouth (Earl)* (1828), 1 Hagg. Ecc. 355, 162 E.R. 611, are distinguishable.[52]

Justice Cullity ultimately finds that there was no duress or coercion under the circumstances of the case before him.

Somewhat curiously, Justice Cullity instead speaks of Mr. Banton as a "willing victim", acknowledging Ms. Yassin as "scheming", but focussing the inquiry into duress on the state of mind of Mr. Banton rather than on Ms. Yassin's intentions:

> In late September and early October in 1994, George Banton had tried to resist Muna's attempts to seduce him into marriage, but in November, he capitulated and consented to it. Although I have also found that marriage was part of Muna's carefully planned and tenaciously implemented scheme to obtain control, and, ultimately, the ownership of his property, as far as the marriage was concerned, he was, at the end, a willing victim. Shortly thereafter he told Victor that he wanted "one last fling".
>
> In view of my finding that George Banton consented to the marriage, it is unnecessary to deal with the questions whether duress makes a marriage void or voidable, and, if the consequence is that the marriage is voidable, whether it can be set aside by anyone other than the parties. I express no opinion on these issues.[53]

Interestingly, Cullity J. draws a significant distinction between the concepts of 'consent' and of 'capacity', finding that a lack of consent neither presupposes nor entails an absence of mental capacity:

> Consent, in the sense in which I have used the term is an act of will. In this sense, it must be distinguished from capacity to marry. Although a lack of mental capacity may be said to vitiate or negative consent, they are obviously different concepts. A lack of consent does not presuppose, or entail, an absence of mental capacity.
>
> A finding of a lack of testamentary capacity does not necessarily determine whether an individual has the mental capacity to marry; nor is testamentary capacity at the time of marriage required before the marriage will revoke a will: *McElroy, Re* (1978), 22 O.R. (2d) 381, 93 D.L.R. (3d) 522 (Ont. Surr. Ct.); *Re Park*, [1953] 2 All E.R. 1411 (C.A.).[54]

---

[52] (1988), 164 D.L.R. (4th) 176 at pp. 222-23, 66 O.T.C. 161 (Gen. Div.).
[53] *Supra*, at p. 223 (D.L.R.).
[54] *Supra*, at p. 224 (D.L.R.).

Having clarified the distinction between 'consent' and 'capacity', Cullity J. emphasizes the low threshold for capacity to marry and finds an absence of evidence that Mr. Banton failed to meet this low standard:

> It is well established that an individual will not have capacity to marry unless he or she is capable of understanding the nature of the relationship and the obligations and responsibilities it involves. . . . There is virtually nothing in the evidence to suggest that George Banton's mental deterioration had progressed to the extent that he was no longer able to pass this not particularly rigorous test.[55]

In finding that Mr. Banton was capable of understanding the nature of the marriage relationship as well as its obligations and responsibilities, Justice Cullity suggests the relevancy of Mr. Banton's previous marriages. In addition, he points to the medical evidence indicating Mr. Banton's acceptance of the marriage.

In enunciating a 'not particularly rigorous' standard for capacity to marry, Cullity J. considers the holdings in *Browning* and *Spier*, discussed above, as well as *Halsbury's* test.[56] In his view, it is unclear whether these three sources, read together, treat capacity to manage property as a necessary condition for capacity to marry:

> Read literally, Sir John Nicholl's statement [that if the capacity be such . . . that the party is incapable of understanding the nature of the contract itself, and incapable, from mental imbecility, to take care of his or her own person and property, such an individual cannot dispose of his or her person and property by the matrimonial contract, any more than by any other contract] appears to have required both incapacity to manage one's self as well as one's property. The passage from *Re Spier* on the other hand [that there must be a capacity to understand the nature of the contract and the duties and responsibilities which it created, and . . . there must also be a capacity to take care of his or her own person and property] can be interpreted as treating incapacity to manage property, by itself, as sufficient to give rise to incapacity to marry. *Halsbury's* statement is, perhaps deliberately, not precise on that question.[57]

Justice Cullity's clear statement that he does not believe that a person incapable of managing property should be found incapable of marriage, may be viewed as a departure from past case law:

---

[55] *Supra*, at p. 224 (D.L.R.).

[56] Halsbury, *Halsbury's Laws of England*, 4th ed. (London: Butterworths, 1974), at para. 911.

[57] *Banton, supra*, footnote 52, at p. 226 (D.L.R.).

> While I believe that it may well be the case that a person who is incapable both with respect to personal care and with respect to property may be incapable of contracting marriage, I do not believe that incapacity of the latter kind should, by itself, have this effect. Marriage does, of course, have an effect on property rights and obligations, but to treat the ability to manage property as essential to the relationship would, I believe, be to attribute inordinate weight to the proprietary aspects of marriage and would be unfortunate. Elderly married couples, whose property is administered for them under a continuing power of attorney, or by a statutory guardian, may continue to live comfortably together. They may have the capacity to make wills and give powers of attorney. I see no reason why this state of affairs should be confined to those who married before incapacity to manage property supervened.[58]

Justice Cullity applies this principle to the facts of *Banton* to find that while Mr. Banton did not have the capacity to manage property, he did have the capacity to marry.

It is important, however, to be aware of the fact that in *Banton*, no direct expert medical evidence was led on the question of capacity to marry. Instead, the experts spoke to the other issues before the court such as testamentary capacity. Given the disparity in applicable capacity standards articulated by Cullity J., this absence is a cause for concern. Arguably, this absence of evidence on the issue of capacity to marry limited the court's ability to arrive at another conclusion.

Justice Cullity appears to have relied on the evidence of Mr. Allen as to Mr. Banton's state of mind at the time of the marriage ceremony:

> Mr. Allen testified that he was aware of the prohibition in the *Marriage Act . . .* of marriages of persons who are "mentally ill." He stated that he had no concerns at all about George Banton's mental condition. He said he remembered George as being "quite a good conversationalist" and there was nothing to indicate that he did not understand the purpose and nature of the ceremony.[59]

Of course, those who preside over marriages often do not have any prior acquaintance with the individuals they marry. It is accordingly difficult for such an individual to make an assessment as to capacity to marry that is in accordance with the requirements under the *Marriage Act*. Only in cases of extreme mental incapacity is it likely that the individual presiding over the marriage will evaluate an

---

[58] *Banton, supra,* footnote 52, at p. 228 (D.L.R.).
[59] *Banton, supra,* footnote 52, at p. 222 (D.L.R.).

individual as incapable of marriage and refuse to perform the marriage on this basis.

One point that the authors urge for consideration is that those vested with the authority to marry should receive some education on the standard for capacity to marry. This is particularly so given that demographic changes suggest that the number of individuals entering into marriage who suffer from some variety of age-related incapacity can only be expected to increase.

In 2003, five years after *Banton*, Greer J.refined the test and application of the capacity to marry in *Sung Estate*.[60]

The facts in *Sung Estate* are as follows. Mr. Sung, recently widowed, married Ms. Feng less than two months after the death of his first wife. Mr. Sung was depressed and lonely and had been diagnosed with cancer. According to the evidence, he was in quite ill-health. While Mrs. Sung was alive, Ms. Feng was hired to clean the house and cook. Shortly before Mrs. Sung's death, Ms. Feng moved into the house to provide full-time care to Mr. Sung.

After Mrs. Sung's death, Mr. Sung and Ms. Feng were quickly married without the knowledge of their children or friends. Mr. Sung died approximately six weeks after the marriage.

The estate and Sung's children sought a declaration that the marriage was *void ab initio*, on the grounds that the deceased, Mr. Sung, lacked the capacity to appreciate and understand the consequences of marriage; in the alternative, they asked that the marriage be declared *void ab initio* because of duress, coercion and undue influence of a degree sufficient to negative any consent that there may have been.

In this case, the marriage ceremony was convened by Reverend E. Kwan who was not a witness at trial, but did provide affidavit evidence. There was no question that the formalities of the marriage accorded with the provisions of the *Marriage Act*. Instead, the question was whether this marriage was *void ab initio*. "It was not a voidable marriage, as neither party prior to Sung's death took steps to have it declared such".[61]

The distinction between a marriage that is *void ab initio* versus one that is *voidable* is relevant to the question of the revocation of any

---

[60] (2003), 1 E.T.R. (3d) 296, 37 R.F.L. (5th) 441 *sub nom. Feng v. Sung Estate* (Ont. S.C.J.), affd 11 E.T.R. (3d) 169, 9 R.F.L. (6th) 229 *sub nom. Feng v. Sung Estate* (C.A.).

[61] *Supra*, at para. 51.

prior will. A marriage that is voidable remains valid until it is voided. In contrast, a marriage that is *void ab initio* is treated as invalid from the outset. This means that where a marriage is found voidable after the death of one of the spouses, the revocation of his or her will by operation of the marriage remains in effect if neither party took steps to void the marriage. A marriage found void *ab initio*, however, will result in a finding that the will was never revoked.

Justice Greer was satisfied on the evidence in this case that the marriage of Mr. Sung and Ms. Feng was *void ab initio*:

> Each case turns on its facts, when it comes to marriages of the infirm, the elderly and the vulnerable. Sung, although only 70 years of age, was both infirm and vulnerable and Feng knew this. The fact that Feng needed money to help support her son (witness the payments from Sung's account to pay for the son's car insurance) and he agreed to pay it, shows his vulnerability. Further, Feng was quite aware of Sung's frail mental and physical health, given her nursing background. It was less than a year after Sung's wife's death that Feng began pressuring Sung. The photos of the two of them together, presented by Feng, show no more affection for Feng that Sung shows for other women in the various photos entered as evidence by the children. These show Sung with his arm around a number of different women at different times. He obviously liked getting his picture taken with his arm around women.
>
> The evidence shows how Feng used both duress and undue influence to force Sung into marriage with her. Normally, parents tell their children and families about forthcoming marriages. Feng clearly prevented this and brought in witnesses whose names she could not even recall. They would therefore have no way of comparing Sung's behaviour at the marriage with his former state of health, nor would they know his family. Feng's evidence that Sung's relatives from Scotland and his goddaughter were told of the forthcoming marriage has no ring of truth to it at all. It is simply another example of Feng's ability to fabricate evidence to support her position. I am satisfied on the evidence that Feng was nothing more than a nurse/housekeeper, who wanted Sung's money, knowing that he was dying, and both impotent and incontinent. The evidence shows that Sung was extremely close to his family members and Feng knew that marriage would disinherit them and give her certain legal rights, because she refused to sign the prenuptial contract.[62]

Accordingly, the marriage certificate was ordered set aside and a declaration was to issue that the marriage was not valid and that Ms.

---

[62] *Supra*, at paras. 53-54.

Feng was not Mr. Sung's legal wife on the date of his death. This given, the will that Mr. Sung made in 1999 remained valid and it was ordered that that will be probated.

Justice Greer also states that had she not found that Mr. Sung was unduly influenced and coerced into his marriage, she would have been satisfied on the evidence that Mr. Sung lacked the mental capacity to enter into the marriage. The test for capacity to marry employed by Greer J. in this regard is the one articulated by Dr. Malloy in *Barrett Estate*: ". . . a person must understand the nature of the marriage contract, the state of previous marriages, one's children and how they may be affected".[63]

While Greer J. does not describe a different test for capacity to marry, and primarily sets aside the marriage in this case on the basis of duress and undue influence, the result in this case is dramatically different from the one in *Banton*. Justice Greer stresses the importance of the unique facts of each case in a determination of this kind.

It is open to interpretation whether the two cases of *Banton* and *Sung Estate*, superficially not dissimilar, differed in outcome primarily because of certain important disparities in the particulars, or because Cullity J. and Greer J. implicitly — if not explicitly — took a different approach to the tests for undue influence, duress and capacity to marry.

The decision of Greer J. was appealed to the Court of Appeal primarily on the issue of whether the trial judge erred in holding that the deceased did not have the capacity to enter into the marriage with Ms. Feng. The Court of Appeal upheld Greer J.'s decision while remarking that the case was a close one. Since the Court of Appeal concluded that it was open to Greer J. to make the finding of incapacity to marry that she did, they did not need to address Greer J.'s other findings relating to fraud, duress and undue influence, nor the issue of whether these would render the marriage only voidable as opposed to void.

As matters stand in Ontario, Greer J.'s decision arguably opens up the possibility of setting aside marriages involving elderly individuals with diminished mental capacity of any variety.

In a recent case from the British Columbia Court of Appeal, *B. (A.) v. D. (C.)*,[64] the question of capacity to form the intention to live

---

[63] *Supra*, at para. 59.

[64] (2009), 94 B.C.L.R. (4th) 38, 66 R.F.L. (6th) 237 (C.A.), leave to appeal to S.C.C. refused October 22, 2009.

separate and apart arose. The court embraced the equivalency between a test for capacity to form the intention to live separate and apart and a test for capacity to marry. In particular, D. Smith J.A., speaking for the court, endorsed Professor Robertson's comments on the subject:

> The reported cases indicate that the test [to marry] is not a particularly demanding one. As was said in the leading English decision, "the contract of marriage is a very simple one, which does not require a high degree of intelligence to comprehend".
> ... Capacity to marry may exist despite incapacity in other legal matters ... Thus, for example, a person may lack testamentary capacity yet have capacity to marry. Similarly, a person may be capable of marrying despite having been declared mentally incompetent and having had a property guardian or guardian of the person appointed.[65]

Specifically, the British Columbia Court of Appeal agreed with Professor Robertson's characterization of the different standards of capacity, acknowledging that his characterization diverged from the standard adopted in the English decisions of *Perry v. Perry*[66] and *Brannan v. Brannan*[67] for the requisite capacity to form the intention to leave a marriage. The court expressed a preference for Professor Robertson's model over the one adopted by the English decisions: "In deciding issues of capacity, to the extent that the law is able to do so, I would endorse an approach that respects the personal autonomy of the individual in making decisions about his or her life".[68]

Future Directions

The authorities discussed thus far stand for the following propositions:

1. capacity to marry is more than a mere appreciation of taking part in a marriage ceremony or a mere understanding of the words invoked;

2. capacity to marry requires an understanding of the nature of the marriage contract;

---

[65] G.B. Robertson, *Mental Disability and the Law in Canada*, 2nd ed. (Toronto: Carswell, 1994), at pp. 253-54, cited in *B. (A.) v. D. (C.)*, *supra*, at para. 22.

[66] [1963] 3 All E.R. 766 (Prob. Div.).

[67] [1973] 1 All E.R. 38 (Fam. Div.).

[68] *B. (A.) v. D. (C.)*, *supra*, footnote 64, at para. 30.

3. to understand the nature of the marriage contract is to understand the duties and responsibilities that normally attach to marriage;
4. the contract of marriage is in essence a simple one, which does not require a high degree of intelligence to comprehend.

Marriage does not have merely social and cultural consequences. In law, marriage operates to revoke a will and to immediately give spouses entitlements to one another's property both during life and upon death. The details of these entitlements have been discussed in previous chapters.

This given, it is a cause for concern that those who are found incapable of managing their property, or of disposing of their property through a will, might still, according to the decision in *Banton*, be capable of marrying. Upon marriage, property consequences of the utmost significance follow: consequences that include creating automatic entitlements to property, revoking any existing will, and replacing any existing will with a spouse's statutory entitlement to the first $200,000 of the estate.

A less rigorous test for capacity to marry allows an individual to do indirectly what he or she has been found incapable of doing directly. This is a fundamental flaw.

The more comprehensive test enunciated in *Browning*, and *Spier* and *Sung Estate* is arguably more appropriate. That is, given the consequences for property that attend marriage, perhaps capacity to marry should require all of the following:

1. capacity to understand the nature of a marriage contract and the duties and responsibilities which it creates;
2. capacity to take care of one's own person; *and*
3. capacity to take care of one's property.

The focus of this chapter has been a review of both historical and current case law on the topic of capacity to marry. After assessing the current test that emerges from a survey of the dicta from the courts, we have suggested one possible alternative direction for the test: a test which may better address the current financial and estate implications of marriage.

CHAPTER 7

CLINICAL AND CONCEPTUAL CONSIDERATIONS

In the previous chapter, case law was surveyed, arriving at the conclusion that there is a tension between the current low threshold for capacity to marry and the financial and estate implications of marriage. A possible adjustment to the test, one which would require capacity to manage one's property in order to marry, was suggested as a possible resolution to the tension. In order to better assess the implications of any suggested directions for change, we must delve into some clinical and conceptual considerations regarding capacity. What are capacity assessments and what do they test? What are the philosophical and conceptual motivations for the criteria used to evaluate capacity? These are the questions that will be answered in this chapter.

Clinical Definitions of Capacity

The Weisstub Inquiry on Mental Competency defines capacity as the ability to make an acceptable informed choice with respect to a specific decision.[1] The emphasis is on functionality and the ability of the person as can be assessed within the context of the decision to be made. Decision-specific competency is the most widely promoted approach, recommended both in the United States and in Ontario. The President's Commission has stated that a person should be considered competent where he or she is capable of communicating pertinent information, possesses a set of values and goals, and possesses the ability to reason about choices.[2] Experts are often called upon to evaluate decision-making goals and values. Of course, the

---

[1] D. Weisstub, *Enquiry on Mental Competency: Final Report* (Toronto: Queen's Printer for Ontario, 1990), at pp. 68-70.
[2] *President's Commission for the Study of Ethical Problems in Medicine and Biomedical and Behavioral Research: Making health care decisions* (Washington, D.C.: U.S. Government Printing Office, 1982).

concept of capacity is intimately connected to the concepts of intention and choice that lie at the core of our legal system.

Historically a global notion of incompetence alluded to a deteriorated mental condition implying an absence of capacity for all tasks. Much like a light bulb, competency was viewed as either all "on" or "off". Given the required clinical severity of the condition, the determination of incompetence was often not difficult. Because such a clinical state occurred late in the course of chronic illness, it left many patients without protection beyond the point when they required it. People often require protective assistance long before they are globally incompetent.

The new definitions of capacity are more restrictive in their scope than the global impairment approach. Restricted notions of capacity segregate capacities according to specific decisions required by defined legal tasks. Where legal tasks are defined, these definitions are either legislated or arise out of the common law. For example, the legal definition (legal criteria) to manage property are given in the *Substitute Decisions Act, 1992*[3] ("*SDA*") whereas the legal definition (legal criteria) for making a will is gleaned from common law cases. The legal criteria are the first step in setting a threshold for determing who is capable or not.

The legal criteria reflect the practical needs of the law. They segregate legal tasks and in this way imply a segregation of mental capacities.[4] The legal criteria determine a restricted notion of competence that recognizes that abilities can be lost in parts. One can be incompetent to manage one's estate and yet competent to make health care decisions. The underlying mental abilities are treated as grouped in non-overlapping categories for the purposes of legal tasks to be distinguished on a cognitive basis. The assumption that different cognitive abilities form non-overlapping categories has yet, however, to be confirmed by research on the subject.

The restricted notion of capacity is valuable clinically in distinguishing those areas in which a person requires protection from those in which they remain capable of making their own decisions. Also, treating competency in a piecemeal fashion can provide protection to an individual sooner than may be afforded under a global notion of competence. The protection provided under this

---

[3] S.O. 1992, c. 30.

[4] D. Checkland and M. Silberfeld, "Reflections on Segregating and Assessing Areas of Competence" (1995), 16 Theorectical Medicine, at pp. 375-88.

approach is also less intrusive since it allows the individual to retain the right to make decisions in certain spheres even where they must relinquish it in others.[5]

In *Starson v. Swayze*,[6] Major J. of the Supreme Court of Canada articulated a two-step test for mental capacity in Ontario. First, a person must be able to understand the information that is relevant to making a treatment decision. Second, a person must be able to appreciate the reasonably foreseeable consequences of the decision or absence of a decision. This requires the patient to be able to apply the relevant information to his or her circumstances, and to be able to weigh the foreseeable risks and benefits of a decision or lack thereof.

Developments in the Definition of Capacity

Reforms in the assessment of capacity have come together with reforms to consent and guardianship statutes. The definition of capacity was clarified and the focus changed from a diagnosis of illness severity to decision-making capacity. The emphasis on preserving autonomy, along with the pressure to keep patients in the community as opposed to institutionalizing them, has been accompanied by a retreat from the notion of global competence. In its place is the idea of partial competency.[7]

In Ontario, the Weisstub Inquiry on Mental Competency endorsed the view "that competency must be understood and evaluated in terms of specific situations or types of decisions".[8] The examination of decision-making is attractive and familiar to the law because of the interplay of this notion with the legally-central notions of intention and choice. The purpose of such a finely circumscribed definition of capacity was to limit the intrusion of the examination of competency to relevant questions only. In this way, autonomy would be preserved, leaving the abilities that did not come to be assessed unchallenged. Those who are found not competent in regard to one or more class of decisions, remain competent with respect to other decisions. The decision or class of decisions to be assessed is

---

[5]   M. Silberfeld, "New Directions in Assessing Mental Competence" (1992), 38 Canadian Family Physician, at pp. 2365-69.

[6]   (2003), 225 D.L.R. (4th) 385, [2003] 1 S.C.R. 722.

[7]   G. Sharpe, "Guardianship: two models for reform" (1983), 4(1) Health Law in Canada, at pp. 13-23 and P. Hommel, L. Wang and J. Bergman, "Trends in Guardianship Reform: implications for the medical and legal professions" (1990), 18(3) Law, Med. and Healthcare, at pp. 213-26.

[8]   Weisstub, *ibid.*, footnote 1, at pp. 68-70.

determined by the nature of the challenge to a person's capacity, the legal definition of capacity, and the functional requirements of the situation.[9]

The global notion of incompetence suggests a degenerative mental condition culminating in a lack of capacity for all mental tasks. On this view, for a person to be found incapable, the underlying medical condition affecting their mental state must be so severe as to impair all mental functions. It was in order to provide protective assistance long before a person is globally incompetent that restricted notions of capacity were proposed. These restricted notions segregate competencies according to specific tasks and reflect the practical needs of the legal process. They also acknowledge that mental abilities can be lost in parts. That is, one can, for example, be incapable of making decisions about the disposition of one's estate and be capable of granting a power of attorney for property. The threshold tests of capacity set out in the *SDA* and the *Health Care Consent Act, 1996*[10] ("*HCCA*") reflect task-specific conceptions of capacity.[11]

In order to reduce institutionalizations, timely community intervention was encouraged. Since it was unanimously agreed that institutionalizing individuals was undesirable, there was also a shift away from the notion of incapacity as final. The *SDA* crystallizes some of these attitudinal shifts by creating a time-limited and potentially reversible notion of incapacity. The *SDA* also provides distinct definitions for all of the following capacities: capacity to manage property, capacity to give a power of attorney for property, capacity to make personal care decisions, and capacity to grant a power of attorney for personal care. In the case of legal guardianship it is now also possible to obtain limited guardianship orders for the management of property and for personal care.

Similar reforms are contained in the *HCCA*. Under the *HCCA*, informed consent requires the person to understand the information that is relevant to making a decision and appreciate the consequences of making or not making a decision. The *HCCA* further specifies other aspects of the decision-making process. For example, a person is entitled to receive certain information in relation to the choice(s) that face him or her. That is, they are entitled to receive the information that a reasonable person in the same circumstances would require in

---

[9]   Silberfeld, *ibid.*, footnote 5, at pp. 2365-69.
[10] S.O. 1996, c. 2, Sch. A.
[11] Silberfeld, *ibid.*, footnote 5, at pp. 2365-69.

order to make a decision about treatment. They are also entitled to responses to requests for additional information. The information contemplated includes a description of the nature of the treatment involved, the expected benefits of the treatment, the material risks of the treatment, the material side-effects of treatment, alternative courses of action, and, the likely consequences of not having treatment. Informed consent must relate to the treatment, must be informed, must be given voluntarily, and must not be obtained through misrepresentation or fraud. Along with these specifications of consent, the *HCCA* provides for omnibus consent: namely, that the definition of consent in the Act applies to all health care Acts provided by all health care practitioners whether or not they belong to a regulated health profession.

The Threshold of Capacity

Medical-legal capacity is a social construct. A finding of incompetence involves a wide variety of considerations, grouped together and applied to a single determination. These considerations include the legal standards of capacity and the decisions of the courts. There are also additional assessment criteria. Evidential standards also inform competency determinations by suggesting relevant questions or avenues of inquiry (evidence gathering), by ordering (logically and temporally) reflection on the evidence once it is gathered, and so on. The capacity thresholds achieved in this way are seldom explicit and may not be uniform. Some matters of degree apply to individual cases and permit a certain degree of flexibility given the circumstances. The legal definitions of capacity create a procedural segregation of capacities. These standards on their own are not, however, sufficient to ensure that a mental deficit in one area will not have ramifications for other capacities as well.[12]

Attempts have been made to compare the thresholds for various segregated capacities. That is, can it be said that the threshold capacity to make one type of decision is lower than the capacity to make another type of decision?[13] Clarification of the different thresholds of capacity would certainly aid in establishing the different legal

---

[12]   Checkland and Silberfeld, *ibid.*, footnote 4, at pp. 375-88.

[13]   M. Silberfeld, *et al.*, "Legal Standards and the Threshold of Competence" (1993), 14 A.Q., at pp. 482-87; M. Silberfeld, D. Stephens and K. O'Rourke, "Cognitive Deficit and Mental Capacity Evaluation" (1994), 13 Can. J. of Aging, at pp. 539-49.

standards for capacity. For example, clarification of the terms 'understanding' and 'appreciation' as used in the definitions of capacity would be helpful. For some, the actual content of a decision is of less import than how the decision was arrived at. Others have felt that the consequences of the decision are critical in determining capacity. Still others stress the requirement of decision authenticity.[14] The failure to identify decision options (where they exist), as well as the inability to understand the consequences of those options, have been found to be strong indicators of incapacity. Regardless of which vision of capacity is preferred; "it is clear that there are degrees of mental capacity. There is a continuum from highly capable to marginally capable and then incapable". Dan Brock has pointed out that the courts in the United States have held that capacity beyond a certain threshold is sufficient to ensure that a person retains decisional authority.[15] In other words, the absence of enough capacity to make a particular decision is a prerequisite for intervention. All of this goes to show that the threshold for capacity is tied to considerations about decisional authority, responsibility, obligation, and intervention. This diversity of relevant considerations renders the line dividing capacity from incapacity imprecise.

Capacity and Competence

Three distinct notions of competence can be distinguished. On the one hand, competence can be viewed as a failure to comply with a common standard of performance. This is the view applied to the detection of disability, and also to the diagnosis of illness. Another perspective is that competence is the maximization of human potential, which may vary greatly from one individual to the next. On this view, the focus is on the development of performance of various kinds, including the development of compensatory strategies for deficits. The final notion of competence depends on the prediction of the need for guardianship. The objective in this case is to establish the point at which legal protection or safeguard is necessary despite the corresponding loss in personal discretion.

The function of capacity assessments in any legislative scheme is to allocate decisional authority. Those who are capable can continue

---

[14]   K. Glass and M. Silberfeld, *Determination of Competence, in Clinical Diagnosis and Management of Alzheimer's Disease*, S. Gauthier, ed. (London, England: Martin Dunitz, 1996), at pp. 331-42.

[15]   D. Brock, "Letter re Elliot" (1992), 3(1) Journal of Clinical Ethics, at p. 88.

to make their own decisions, while those who are incapable require a surrogate decision-maker (or some other protection). Capacity assessment therefore serves two goals: to protect decisional autonomy for some individuals and to identify the need for the protection of other individuals from harm.[16]

The notion of mental competence involves both "purely cognitive" and "functional" aspects. What is at stake is a person's capacity to do certain things. In this way, mental competence is a complex ability. To assess mental competence, a variety of abilities may need to be mentioned. Since abilities are generally what is called 'dispositional states', no single act establishes with assurance the presence or absence of the ability.[17]

Related to mental competence is the notion of rationality in decision-making. There are two general approaches to defining such rationality:

(i) the psychosocial approach, and
(ii) decision analysis.

The psychological approach to rationality focuses on the impediments to reasonable choice that arise from bad judgment and the universal inclination toward self-deception. Another approach, namely decision analysis, focuses on the scope of choice and involves an explicit weighing of the inherent uncertainties of all alternatives.

The psychosocial approach involves understanding a person's choices in terms of their own psychology as it exists within the context of their personal history. As such, the scope of considerations can be very broadly defined. The considerations include:

(i)   the nature and severity of the cerebral dysfunction;
(ii) the person's reaction to the deficit; and
(iii) the cumulative effect of (i) and (ii) on interpersonal or psychosocial adjustment.

Sometimes a wider scope is proposed including:

(i)   social interaction and resources;
(ii) personal coping and well-being; and
(iii) environmental fit. Problems in measurement result from the wide scope of considerations.

---

[16] Glass and Silberfeld, *ibid.,* footnote 14, at pp. 331-42.
[17] D. Checkland and M. Silberfeld, "Competence and the Three 'A's': autonomy, authenticity and aging" (1993), 12(4) Can. J. of Aging, at pp. 453-68.

Decision analysis defines a standard of rationality and as such involves procedures such as eliciting preferred outcomes within the domain of all possible outcomes in a given context, assigning values to each particular outcome, assessing the subjective (or objective) possibility of each outcome, considering the risk-taking propensity of the individual, and contemplating certain factors external to the individual making the choice (for example, economic cost to society).[18]

Capacity and Autonomy

For the purposes of the present analysis, the authors have defined autonomy to mean liberty of decision and action. This includes freedom from constraint and coercion. With autonomy one can act, or decide, according to one's intentions, wishes, preferences and values.[19] There are two uses of autonomy:

(i)   the normative use, where "autonomy" refers to a general right to non-interference which a person possesses (given certain conditions); and

(ii) a weaker use where "autonomy" can be equated simply with the absence of interference (one common sense of "freedom").

The law pulls together two apparently distinct questions:

(i)   whether a person is competent, and

(ii) whether we should respect that person's decisions.[20]

In other words, the question of a person's competence or incompetence settles the question of whether a person retains decisional authority under the law.

A further distinction is relevant, namely, autonomy as a psychological capacity. Autonomy refers to a "capacity and disposition to make choices in a rational manner . . . in the absence of certain particular attitudes and inner obstacles, such as blind acceptance of tradition and authority, neurotic compulsions, and the like".[21] "We might define the autonomy of persons in terms of the autonomy of

---

[18] M. Silberfeld, "Social Competence in Cognitive Disorder", in *Prospects in Aging*, L. Abisch, ed. (Sandoz: Academic Press, 1993), at pp. 163-203.

[19] K. Madigan and M. Silberfeld, "Clinical Application of the Least Restrictive Alternative in Competency Assessments" (1993), 12 E.T.P.J., at pp. 282-92.

[20] Brock, *ibid.*, footnote 15, at p. 88.

[21] T.E.J. Hill, *Autonomy and Self-Respect* (New York: Cambridge University Press, 1991).

those psychological states".[22] On this conception, the most fundamental notion is that of an autonomous act or choice. In this way, psychological autonomy becomes either a necessary or sufficient condition for making choices recognized by the law.

Another way of thinking about the issue is in terms of control: "We think of autonomy as requiring, whatever else, that a person be in control of her life".[23] For Haworth and others such as Gerald Dworkin, autonomy is the capacity to assume reflective attitudes, that is to reflect upon and evaluate, our desires, beliefs, and actions.[24] These reflective attitudes can also be thought of as 'second-order' desires, that is desires about desires. These second-order desires may correspond to what lawyers call 'due deliberation'. In this way, there may be a tendency to "take too narrowly cognitivist a view of the way in which a commitment to certain things may be clarified".[25] For example, a person's verbal skills, energy, or motivation to communicate may wane without affecting, or in any case compromising, his or her autonomy. But, if a cognitive threshold of competence can be clearly delineated, the law's needs can be satisfied. "Persons with 'autonomous' beliefs and values, but who lacked the ability to translate these into choices, would not be possible candidates for autonomy".[26]

Autonomy connects an individual to his or her commitments and allows an individual to actively define him or herself.[27] In this way the concepts of ownership and authenticity are also engaged in the notion of autonomy. An autonomous individual identifies with or possesses his or her actions; this much seems closely connected with our conception of individuals as agents. Understood in this way, undue influence and coercion are anethema in their ability to deny ownership of a person's actions.

Donald Davidson describes ownership of actions in this way: "For most people most of the time we can explain (and sometimes

---

[22] R. Double, "Two Types of Autonomy Account" (1992), 22(1) Can. J. of Philosophy, at pp. 65-80.

[23] L. Haworth, *Autonomy: an essay in psychology and ethics* (New Haven: Yale University Press, 1986), at p. 133.

[24] G. Dworkin, *The Theory and Practice of Autonomy* (New York: Cambridge University Press, 1988).

[25] R. Young, "Autonomy and the 'Inner Self'" (1980), 17 American Philosophical Quarterly 35-43, at p. 37; Dworkin, *ibid.*, at p. 17.

[26] Double, *ibid.*, footnote 22, at p. 67.

[27] Dworkin, *ibid.,* footnote 24, at p. 26.

predict) their behaviour by ascribing to them beliefs, desires, and other attitudes which can be traced to no further origin and which exhibit no pathological characteristics".[28] Exceptions to ownership include certain recognizable attitudes and inner obstacles, such as delusions, which may define what is alien to a person. An "inner obstacle" will be some state that prevents a person from enacting his or her highest preference at a given time. Even a felt desire can be alien to a person. The person may "have" the desire but reject it or disapprove of it. In such cases, the person "places the rejected desire outside of the scope of his preferences, so that it is not a candidate for satisfaction at all".[29] In contrast to such internal obstacles are external obstacles that may constitute undue influence or coercion.

Another way in which to view authenticity is as an expression arising from enduring character. That is, an authentic act expresses who one is in a deep or revealing way. It would be hard to exaggerate the importance to our concept of a person of the existence of relatively enduring character states or dispositions. People do change. But the concept of such change can only be measured and identified against a backdrop of enduring character.[30] A person's past will often leave traces or 'authentic residues' of a previous autonomy or competence. We must respect this enduring authenticity, but at the same time be careful not to use the existence of long-standing states of character as a way of restricting learning, growth, or other change. It is possible for a person to be a "prisoner of authenticity", unable to have perspective on, or to constrain, long-standing traits. Dependency is one example of an inability to constrain a long-standing trait.

Capacity and Wishes

To promote autonomy is to take wishes seriously. Wishes are to be upheld wherever possible in order to support autonomy and the choices of individuals. To do so requires ongoing consultation, regardless of the extent of incapacity or diminished cognition or ability. Agency and choice are central to legal decision-making.

It is important to distinguish wishes from choices. Wishes are valuable because they are desired. They are not subject to logic or

---

[28] D. Davidson, "Knowing One's Own Mind", *Proceedings and Addresses of the American Philosophical Association* (1987), 61, at pp. 441-54.

[29] H. Frankfurt, *The Importance of What We Care About* (New York: Cambridge University Press, 1988), at p. 66.

[30] D. Checkland and M. Silberfeld, *ibid.*, footnote 17, at p. 464.

criticism.[31] Wishes are immune from judgment about the priority of one wish over another. Wishes also transparently show the disjunction between desire and interests. Simple wishes do not allow for wider interests. Wishes are effortless like emotions. Wishes do not distinguish humans from other forms of life. Wishes disregard the possibility of ambivalence and possible self-deception. Very often wishes reflect the avoidance of responsibility for making a choice. And simple wishes almost invariably fail to allow for reciprocal forbearance. With wishes, the strength of felt desire has no secure correlation with how well-off one ends up.[32] Since desires cannot be improved upon without information processing and judgment, simple wishes lack the authority that attaches to values.[33]

While this is a definition of wishes that the authors adopt for the purposes of this book, it does not appear to be the definition embraced in the *HCCA* which states that,

> 5. (1) A person may, while capable, express wishes with respect to treatment, admission to a care facility or a personal assistance service.
>
> . . . . .
>
> (3) Later wishes expressed while capable prevail over earlier wishes.

The use of the word 'wishes' in these two provisions is potentially inconsistent with the distinction we wish to draw.

However, the use of the word 'wishes' in the following provisions of the *SDA* is consistent with our view that incapable people continue to have wishes:

> 17. (5) The Public Guardian and Trustee shall consider the incapable person's current wishes, if they can be ascertained, and the closeness of the applicant's relationship to the person.
>
> . . . . .
>
> 18. (4) The court shall take into consideration the incapable person's current wishes, if they can be ascertained, and the closeness of the applicant's relationship to the person.

To act on simple wishes is not valuable in and of itself unless such action furthers the person's interests. There is no private self-

---

[31] J. Elster, *Sour Grapes. Edition de la maison des sciences de l'homme* (Paris: Cambridge University Press, 1993).

[32] J. Griffin, *Against the Taste Model, in Interpersonal Comparisons of Well-Being*, J. Elster and J.E. Roemer, eds. (New York: Cambridge University Press, 1991), at pp. 45-69.

[33] H. Frankfurt, "Freedom of Will and the Concept of a Person" (1971), 68 J. of Philosophy, at pp. 5-20.

regarding wish-fulfillment: every action affects the external world including other individuals within it.[34] Respect for a person is shown through an examination of his or her motives and attitudes even when such an examination does not culminate in granting the person's wishes. It is this consideration that is required to respect human agency and the doctrine of mental capacity. In most cases, a person's choices do not perfectly reflect their wishes. Forming a wish is only the first step to making the kind of considered choice that the law recognizes as capable. If wishes were sufficient as a basis for legal action, there would be no need for capacity assessments: we all have wishes. What the concept of capacity acknowledges is that more goes into a capable choice than mere wishes. Successful social adaptation allows wider interests to prevail over wishful subjectivity. If wishes were choices, we would all be beggars.

Based on this distinction between wishes and choices, we can see that the notion of capacity is based on making choices. Information must be processed, understood and appreciated.

The wish to get married can be a wish without further consideration. The wish to have a baby is distinct from the desire to raise a child. In a similar vein, an incapable person's wish to marry can be void of other relevant considerations. Such an exclusionary wish can exist in a person who is incapable of implementing marriage as a choice — that is, incapable of participating in any of the arrangements and legalities of marriage. Such wishful thinkers depend on others to fulfill their wish to marry and are subsequently subject to undue influence and coercion.

To recognize the potential for an incapable wish requires considerable skill in many instances. There are people who can express wishes and are at the same time incapable or at least unable to satisfy others of their capacity when their wishes have come into doubt.

Capacity and Risk

In a liberal democratic society people lead their lives according to the choices they make. The state has a limited role in the personal affairs of individuals. Until recently, the interventions of the state have been limited to property matters (where the law is well- practiced). More recently, however, the state has taken a protective interest in health care and personal care decisions. The interests of the state in

---

[34]   S.L Hurley, *Natural Reasons* (New York: Oxford University Press, 1989).

health care and personal care decisions have gone quite far, as demonstrated in the *SDA* and the *HCCA*. Freedom of choice is the hallmark of liberty; it is the cornerstone of western liberal democratic societies such as our own. Nevertheless, our commitment to decisional autonomy does not and should not blind us to the recognition that protectionism is warranted in the proper circumstances. For all his promotion of decisional liberty, J.S. Mill allowed that, "[it] is, perhaps, hardly necessary to say that this doctrine is meant to apply only to human beings in the maturity of their faculties. We are not speaking of children. Those in a state to require being taken care of by others must be protected from their own actions as well as against external injury".[35] Finding the delicate balance between the preservation of autonomy and beneficent intervention is difficult. Despite the potential pitfalls, the law creates a threshold test for capacity that draws a line between those who require protection and those who can function on their own.

The law presumes a person is capable, yet persons are brought for assessment on the opposite presumption. Often it is not clear whose interest is being served by the assessment. The assessment can imperil a person who does not need it by putting them at risk of improperly losing some freedom of choice. Studies on pre-screening capacity assessments have demonstrated that many requested capacity assessments are not required.[36] Capacity assessments are not required under the following circumstances:

(i)   protection is not required;
(ii)   a capacity assessment is the wrong legal avenue for addressing the problem;
(iii)   a less restrictive solution exists;
(iv)   there is a mistaken expectation of the outcome;
(v)   the assessment is carried out even when there is no assent to it;[37] or
(vi)   there is no appropriate substitute decision-maker available.

Who can challenge another's capacity? Under what circumstances is it justifiable to submit someone to an examination of capacity?

---

[35] J.S. Mill, *On Liberty*, H.B. Acton, ed. (London: J.M. Dent and Sons, 1972).

[36] M. Silberfeld, M. Finstad and B. Dickens, "Prescreening Competency Assessments" (1993), 26(3) Annals The Royal College of Physicians and Surgeons of Canada, at pp. 165-68.

[37] See the decision in *Koch (Re)*, [1997] 33 O.R. (3d) 485, 70 A.C.W.S. (3d) 712 (Gen. Div.).

Because uniform, accepted criteria for the assessment of capacity do not as yet exist, examining capacity poses certain risks. Since assessments involve people coming under scrutiny in situations of perceived risk, examiners can at times set a standard for tasks higher than those required in everyday life. Yet a person who can function satisfactorily in day-to-day life should not be found incapable.

People come to be assessed when their capacity is questioned by others. Seldom do they seek an assessment of themselves. Where a person seeks an assessment for him or herself, it is usually under circumstances where they have been declared incapable and want to have their decisional freedom restored.[38] Otherwise, an assessment hinges on the perception of another or others that the person for whom the assessment is requested is at risk. Caregivers often have to balance competing interests and interested parties in choosing whether or not to request a formal capacity assessment. Caregivers should be clear about whose interest they are serving in requesting a formal assessment of capacity. Usually, an assessment should only be requested where it will be in the best interests of the person assessed. The only exception to this is under cirucmstances of a supervening legal requirement to request an assessment for the good or protection of another or others.[39]

Informally and without the use of any rigorous criteria, people, especially caregivers, assess the performance of others every day and in a variety of ways. Health care professionals informally assess a person's ability to consent to treatment. Lawyers informally assess a person's capacity to instruct them. Family members informally assess a parent's capacity to live independently. If, under such circumstances, an individual becomes concerned about a person's performance, they may choose to take the next step and request a formal assessment of capacity. There should be a sufficiently high perception of risk after an informal assessment of lack of capacity to justify a formal assessment that may precipitate a legal or medical conflict.[40]

The perception and assessment of risk is complex. Two considerations usually arise: how likely is a bad outcome, and how bad will it be? Often these two considerations are not sufficiently

---

[38] M. Silberfeld, *et al.*, "Capacity Assessments for Requests to Restore Legal Competence" (1995), 10(4) Int'l J. of Geriatric Psychiatry, at pp. 191-97.

[39] S. Verma and M. Silberfeld, "Approaches to Capacity and Competency: the Canadian view" (1997), 20(1) Int'l J. of Law and Psychiatry, at pp. 35-46.

[40] *Ibid.*, at pp. 35-46.

distinguished. For example, it may come to someone's attention that the cognitive abilities of an elderly person in the community are failing. This person may have been involved in several incidents of unsafe practices, such as using potentially dangerous household appliances in an unsafe way. For example, the improper use of a gas oven could lead to a damaging explosion. However, it may also be the case that the oven is used only infrequently. The individual in question may also have declared that he or she would no longer use the gas oven. In the past, the person may have been unable to keep such promises. Here, the consequences of an error must be balanced against the likelihood that it will or will not occur. It is also important to keep in mind which individuals will likely be affected by the bad outcome. For the elderly woman running out of financial resources, placement in some assisted-living facility may be the better outcome from the viewpoint of the caregivers. From the woman's perspective this may be a very bad outcome. Since risk involves assessing the likelihood of certain occurrences and unwanted consequences, risk assessment changes depending on the perspective of the assessment. In this way, it is important to keep in mind that when it comes to assessing risk, caregivers are often in a position of conflict with those under their care.

It is useful to think of risk in three ways that can be distinguished: The actuarial, the clinical, and, the subjective.[41] The actuarial framework assumes the existence of meaningful frequency tables relating to the relevant occurrences. Even when some data does exist, for example, the data collected by insurance companies for their particular purposes, deeper questions remain. While an actuarial rate may be useful for the design of general policies of health care, when we are concerned with the welfare of an individual, it is not clear in what way statistical generalities apply. Every individual belongs to many different classes. In spite of this, a single 'judgment' must be made. What consequences are "bad"? How bad are they? Even the choice of events to be evaluated can be controversial. There can be a clash of perceptions about which events are serious. What one person views as a "failure to acknowledge risk" may from another perspective be better characterized as a different perception of risk. Caregivers find it reassuring and authoritative to speak of their views of risk as if there were actuarial data to support them. In fact, this is seldom the case.

---

[41] M. Silberfeld, "The Use of 'Risk' in Decision-Making" (1992), 11(2) Can. J. of Aging, at pp. 124-36.

Clinical judgments of risk are made by experts about the eventual course of an illness.[42] Usually they are based on shared experience, such as textbooks and academic papers, and on studies conducted on selected disease populations. There have been recent attempts to quantify those experiences.[43] These studies show that clinical judgment is most often grounded in the professional experience of the practitioner.[44] The judgment reflects the nature of the illness and the caregiver's responsibility. It also reflects the nature of the practitioner's practice.

People believe they know what they want and do not want. This is the subjective perspective on risk. Most often the focus in any risk assessment is the avoidance of undesirable events. These subjective perspectives can be unstable especially during illness. Risk perspectives are influenced by optimism or pessimism, depression, pain, and by fluctuating lucidity. The psychodynamics of risk depend on hopes, fears of loss, and perceived entitlements.[45] Some normative pressures, such as laws, other societal regulations, or the actions of interested groups, may influence people's risk perception. For the patient, the normative considerations may force a compromise.[46]

Capacity Assessments

As previously mentioned, mental capacity is decision, time and situation specific. Mental capacity assessment involves understanding and appreciating the basis for decision-making. This basis has an extensive reach. Here is a way to try and tie it together.

Understanding a decision includes eliciting and identifying the decisional options available. Missing options should be suggested. When the options are recognized, their pertinence and the reasons for them clarified, the preferred option can be understood. The risks and benefits of a preferred option should be known insofar as they impact

---

[42] J. Balla, *The Diagnostic Press: a model for clinical teachers* (New York: Cambridge University Press, 1985).

[43] A. Feinstein, *Clinimetrics* (New Haven: Yale University Press, 1987).

[44] J. Groopman, *How Doctors Think* (Boston: Houghton Mifflin Co., 2007).

[45] M. Silberfeld, "Hope, Loss and Entitlement: Lessons from the Oncology Situation" (1981), 26 Can. J. of Psychiatry, at pp. 415-18; M. Silberfeld, "The Psychology of Hope and the Modifications of Entitlement Near the End of Life", in *Attitudes of Entitlement: theoretical and clinical issues*, V. Volkan and T.C. Rogers, eds. (Charlottesville: University of Virginia Press, 1988).

[46] M. Silberfeld, *et al.*, "Choosing a Risky Treatment; Psychosocial Aspects of Risky Choice" (1988), 13(1) Psychiatry Journal, at pp. 9-11.

on the person's life. The subjective view of risk of the preferred option should be stated. The risks of discarded options are preferably known as well. Once identified, the risks should be voluntarily assumed.[47] Preferences for a decisional option are statements of important beliefs. These beliefs are an indication of values which 'stand for the person' and can include religious and cultural values. Although those values are often longstanding, values can also be altered by the circumstances that lead to an assessment. Since decision-making takes time, some assessments may occur in the midst of an incomplete decision-making process. In the absence of time pressure, the inability to complete a decision may itself be a symptom of a greater disturbance. Where possible, time should be allowed for an assessment to take place over a number of interviews.

Appreciating the consequences of a decision at its most general involves a recognition of the impact on the person's life. The consequences are appreciated with reference to the person's life history and aspirations. They are connected to value statements. However, in expressing his or her values, a person is expected to go beyond a simple statement of wishes. Some anticipation of the future, and the ability to consider events which have not occurred or may not occur, are necessary.[48] Furthermore, in order to appreciate the implications of a choice, a person may need to apply reflective thought, also known as higher-order intentions, to show due deliberation, prudence in the circumstances, to restrain themselves from impulsiveness, and to avoid certain biases. It is helpful for the assessment if the person can recognize his or her own limitations in making the decision at hand. Once a limitation is recognized, the person should be able to explain how they are compensating for it.[49]

Diagnostic and clinical information about disabilities, such as cognitive deficits of various kinds, show whether the decision made is supported or eliminated by the biological substrate. An incapable decision must be shown to depend for its occurrence on an inability to understand and appreciate. While diagnosis of a disability does not in itself indicate capacity or incapacity, knowledge of such a diagnosis

---

[47] Silberfeld, *ibid.,* footnote 41, at pp. 124-36.
[48] K. Glass and M. Silberfeld, *ibid.,* footnote 14, at pp. 331-42.
[49] M. Silberfeld, W. Corber and D. Checkland, "Acknowledgement of Limitations and Understanding of their Consequences in Mental Capacity Assessments" (1995), 13(3) Behaviourial Sciences and the Law, at pp. 381-90.

may assist the assessor(s) to make a proper determination that a given choice is not wanton, or accidental, or influenced by others.

It is the task of the assessor to pull all these considerations together, assign to each piece of information its due, and come to a final decision. The legal standard for the capacity in question must be heeded in making this decision: knowledge of specific statutes or case law may be indispensable in certain instances.

With this in mind, a proposed model for capacity assessment is presented. This model has two components of information gathering: the core and the modal. Also central to this model is the act of making a final capacity determination based on the information gathered.[50]

What is referred to as the core aspect applies to all assessments in the same way. It includes information reflecting the individual's cognitive functioning, social functioning, and other factors related to medical status or illness that could influence decision-making.

CORE

1. Mental status
2. Cognitive function
3. Social functioning
4. Other factors related to choice

---

[50] M. Silberfeld, *ibid.,* footnote 18, at pp. 163-203.

The modal part of the examination is tailored to the particular decision that is being challenged and for which the person is being assessed. The decision itself and the choice of decision are examined. The legal standard required for those kinds of decisions is applied. Legal standards and decisions made by courts provide a general guideline.[51] The patient's preferences, values, ability to recognize alternative choices, to appreciate trade-offs, and his or her history of risk-taking are then considered. Corroborating information is obtained with consent where available.

MODAL

1. Specific decisions
2. Legal standards
3. Decision- making
   a. preferences
   b. values
   c. alternative choices
   d. trade-offs
   e. risk-taking

What is called the 'inferential leap' is coming to a judgment with respect to the information gathered. The judgment ties together the core and modal parts into an 'all things considered' opinion about capacity. It is a dichotomous opinion: capable or incapable. From the accumulated list of deficits, experts make inferences about decision-

---

[51] P. Appelbaum, and T. Grisso, "Assessing Patients' Capacities to Consent to Treatment" (1988), 319 New England J. of Med., at pp. 1635-38.

making. The underlying capacities corresponding to the ability to make certain choices are not necessarily known. It is unclear which deficits implicate certain choices. The inferential leap is a judgment call, and depends to a certain extent on the expert making the decision. This inferential leap should also clarify the knowledge base upon which the opinion is rendered.

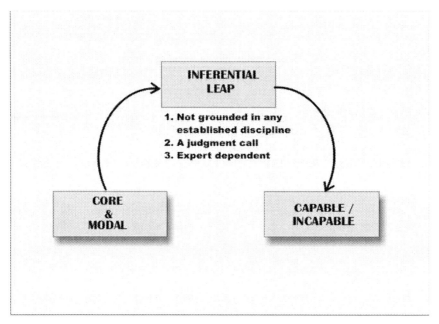

Capacity Presumptions

The law starts with the presumption that all persons have the capacity to make decisions about their own lives and to execute these decisions, unless they are found to be incapable. The presumption of capacity comes for the common law's recognition of the individual's right to liberty and to autonomy. The right to liberty and autonomy was further protected when the law progressed from the conception of global capacity to one of segregated capacities. The "least restrictive alternative" principle leads to the notion of partial capacity and encourages alternatives to the imposition of protection that totally restricts liberty. Instead, less intrusive solutions that minimize the loss of autonomy are preferred. Segregated definitions of capacity permit persons to be found incapable in a restricted area while retaining their discretionary authority in all other areas of decision-making. A further refinement on the definitions of capacity has made findings of incapacity time-limited or reversible where warranted by the person's condition.[52]

A presumption plays a specific role in forming an opinion about capacity. The presumption is compelling when the evidence is inconclusive. A presumption points towards one of two mutually exclusive conclusions, acting as a tie-breaker. This applies both to the law and to clinicians. The presumption directs the assessor to find the person capable unless and until there is credible evidence to the contrary.[53]

The presumption of capacity plays a screening role. The general presumption that a person is capable, as articulated in *Kahn v. St. Thomas Psychiatric Hospital*,[54] places the burden on the individual questioning the capacity of another to support his or her assertion. In order to meet this onus, the person asserting incapacity must provide a credible basis for the existence of risk. No one has a general right to question or assess another's capacity on the basis of speculation, no matter how well-intentioned the questioner may be. A presumption does not address the question of the appropriate threshold of capacity (how well a person must do measured against stated criteria) or the question of how strongly an opinion must be backed by available evidence to be warranted.[55]

The legal presumptions are practically important for those who assess capacity. When confronted with mental incapacity, mental health professionals must strive to implement effective interventions while simultaneously respecting the person's autonomy. The assessing professional must be sensitive to the capacity concerns about protection of incapable persons and respect for their autonomy and privacy rights. Promotion of the least restrictive alternative requires the clinician to seek that intervention alternative which, while effective and protective, minimizes interference with the individual's liberty of decision and action. Clinicians must balance the incapable person's need for protection from the consequences of their incapable decisions and actions against the need to be respected as a person. All assessments commence with the presumption of capacity. This

---

[52] S. Verma and M. Silberfeld, *ibid.*, footnote 39, at pp. 35-46.

[53] K. Madigan, D. Checkland and M. Silberfeld, "Presumptions Respecting Mental Competence" (1994), 39(3) Can. J. of Psychiatry, pp. 147-52.

[54] (1992), 87 D.L.R. (4th) 289, 7 O.R. (3d) 303 at p. 316 (C.A.), leave to appeal to S.C.C. refused 93 D.L.R. (4th) vii, 75 C.C.C. (3d) vii.

[55] Madigan, Checkland and Silberfeld, *ibid.,* footnote 53.

benefits the person assessed by affirming his or her autonomy until and unless incompetence has been positively established by credible evidence. The presumption of capacity requires the assessor to justify his or her judgment of incapacity by resort to credible evidence. The burden of persuasion is on the assessor.[56]

The clinical and conceptual considerations discussed above provide insight into capacity to marry. It is ultimately these considerations that can guide us to an informed choice about whether the present approach to the capacity to marry or to the financial and estate consequences of marriage should be revisited.

---

[56] K. Madigan and M. Silberfeld, *ibid.*, footnote 19.

CHAPTER 8

CONCLUSIONS

In the foregoing chapters, the authors have examined capacity to marry through a variety of lenses: demographic, historical, clinical, conceptual, through foundational legal comments, and through the dicta of the courts. What emerges from this examination is an unequivocal message that the law as it stands is unclear.

It is clear from the foregoing examination that in order to marry, a person ought to understand the nature of the marriage relationship and its responsibilities. However, the scope of this understanding is variably defined. Is an understanding of the marriage relationship and responsibilities limited to an understanding of the emotional bond of marriage? Or is a more rigorous and complete understanding required, one which includes an understanding of the financial, estate and property consequences that accompany marriage? If all who wished to enter into marriage were required to pass a test on the legal implications of marriage under the *Family Law Act*, the *Divorce Act* and the *Succession Law Reform Act*, perhaps marriage rates would see a sharp decline!

The statement that "the contract of marriage is a very simple one" as deduced from preceding case law, belies the suggestion that a high level of understanding of the consequences of marriage is required. As a result of this statement from the courts, the test for the capacity to marry has been held to be much less stringent than the one for testamentary capacity or capacity to manage property. The result of this is that where a person is incapable of making or revoking a will, and one has been found incapable of managing one's own financial affairs, this will not preclude the person from entering into the contract of marriage. The further implication of this state of affairs is that a person may do indirectly what one cannot do directly: one may revoke a will through the act of marriage, when one cannot revoke it otherwise.

From the preceding analysis in *Banton v. Banton*,[1] Cullity J. rejected an interpretation of the old English case of *Browning v.*

Reane[2] that would require capacity to manage property as a prerequisite for marriage. Sir John Nicholl's remarks in that case were as follows:

> If the incapacity be such . . . that the party is incapable of understanding the nature of the contract itself, and incapable, from mental imbecility, to take care of his or her own person and property, such an individual cannot dispose of her person and property by the matrimonial contract, any more than by any other contract.[3]

Instead, Cullity J. chose to limit the applicability of the sentiment expressed above and to find that the inability to manage one's property would not automatically preclude capacity to marry:

> While I believe that it may well be the case that a person who is incapable both with respect to personal care and with respect to property may be incapable of contracting marriage, I do not believe that incapacity of the latter kind should, by itself, have this effect. Marriage does, of course, have an effect on property rights and obligations, but to treat the ability to manage property as essential to the relationship would, I believe, be to attribute inordinate weight to the proprietary aspects of marriage and would be unfortunate. Elderly married couples whose property is administered for them under a continuing power of attorney, or by a statutory guardian, may continue to live comfortably together. They may have capacity to make wills and give powers of attorney. I see no reason why this state of affairs should be confined to those who married before incapacity to manage property supervened.[4]

Justice Cullity's reluctance to "attribute inordinate weight to the proprietary aspects of marriage" is understandable when analyzing the case in its entirety. Marriage does mean many things that are quite independent of purely financial considerations. However, whether rightly or wrongly, the law as it stands does put great weight on the proprietary aspects of marriage by attaching to marriage a whole slew of financial implications. We ignore this reality at our peril.

As a conclusion of the foregoing analysis, there are at least two potential avenues to redress the inconsistency between the financial implications that accompany marriage and the lack of consideration given to these financial implications by the existing threshold for capacity to marry. Either the tie between marriage and significant

---

[1]   (1988), 164 D.L.R. (4th) 176, 66 O.T.C. 161 (Gen. Div.).
[2]   (1812), 161 E.R. 1080, [1803-13] All E.R. Rep. 265.
[3]   *Supra*, at p. 266 (All E.R.).
[4]   *Banton, supra,* footnote 1, at p. 228 (D.L.R.).

testamentary and property implications should be broken or relaxed under circumstances of mental decline, or the threshold for capacity to marry should be raised.

If indeed it is desirable, as Cullity J. indicates that it is, not to attribute inordinate weight to the proprietary aspects of marriage, then perhaps such significant proprietary consequences should not attach to marriage and a new regime be devised to address the incumbent risks raised. Currently, a multitude of proprietary implications follow upon marriage: marriage revokes a will; spouses are entitled to a preferential share of an estate on intestacy; and married spouses are entitled to an equalization payment upon dissolution of the marriage that evens out both parties' net family properties upon emerging from the relationship. Those without capacity to make a new will in contemplation of marriage or subsequent to marriage may still be deemed to have the requisite capacity to enter into marriage and the attendant consequences thereto. These legislated entitlements combined place profound weight on the proprietary aspects of marriage which when tested by capacity issues cause potential undesired and undetermined results.

Given the issues raised, the question of whether marriage and proprietary entitlements should be intimately intertwined is beyond the scope of this book. What the authors wish to emphasize is that a test for capacity to marry that allows an individual without capacity to manage his or her own property and without testamentary capacity to enter into marriage cannot be reconciled with the existing financial and testamentary implications that automatically accompany the contract of marriage.

It is our hope that through our exploration of the relevant fundamental concepts, the historical development of the law, and the current state of the law, we have provided a solid foundation upon which to approach the resolution of the existent tension.

Until a resolution is reached, all those with diminished mental capacity will remain vulnerable to exploitation through marriage. This is likely to become an increasingly pressing question as the aged proportion of the population, who are particularly prone to declines in mental capacity, is expected to sharply rise in the future.

As Professor Oosterhoff concludes in his article, "Consequences of a January/December Marriage: a Cautionary Tale",[5] "on these

---

[5]   A.H. Oosterhoff, "Consequences of a January/December Marriage: a Cautionary Tale" (1999), 18 E.T.P.J. 261-284, at p. 284.

issues, the law needs to be brought into line with modern realities". This is a position for which the authors of this book would advocate. The sooner the disparity between the development of the concept of capacity to marry in the common law with capacity requirements relating to property is acknowledged and addressed, the better off we all will be.

BIBLIOGRAPHY

Aaron, H.J., "Longer Life Spans: Boon or Burden?" (2006), 135 Daedalus, vol. 1, at pp. 9-19

Appelbaum, P., and T. Grisso, "Assessing Patients' Capacities to Consent to Treatment" (1988), 319 New England J. of Med., at pp. 1635-38

Ascher, M.L., "Curtailing Inherited Wealth" (1990), 89 Mich. L. Review 69

Balla, J., *The Diagnostic Press: a model for clinical teachers* (New York: Cambridge University Press, 1985)

Beaupré, P., "I do . . . Take two? Changes in intentions to remarry among divorced Canadians during the past 20 years", Statistics Canada, Analytical Studies, July 17, 2007, available online: www.statcan.gc.ca

Bentham, J., "Principles of the Civil Code", in E. Dupont, ed.; R. Hildreth, trans., *Theory of Legislation*, vol. 1 (Boston: Weeks, Jordan & Co., 1840)

Berkman, L.F., and M.M. Glymour, "How Society Shapes Aging: The Centrality of Variability" (2006), 135 Daedalus, vol. 1, at pp. 105-114

Boyd, M., and A. Li, "May-December: Canadians in age-discrepant relationships", Statistics Canada article (2003), No. 70, at pp. 29-33

Brock, D., "Letter re Elliot" (1992), 3(1) Journal of Clinical Ethics, at p. 88

CBC News, March 9, 2005, Statistics Canada Report, available online at: http://www.cbc.ca/news/background/marriage/

CBC News, January 14, 2008, available online at: http://www.cbc.ca/canada/story/2008/01/14/death-stats.html

Chambers, L., *Married Women and Property Law in Victorian Ontario* (Toronto: University of Toronto Press, 1997)

Checkland, D., and M. Silberfeld, "Reflections on Segregating and Assessing Areas of Competency" (1995), 16 Theorectical Medicine, at pp. 375-88

Checkland, D., and M. Silberfeld, "Competence and the Three 'A's": autonomy, authenticity and aging" (1993), 12(4) Can. J. of Aging, at pp. 453-68

Clark, W., and S. Crompton, "Till death do us part? The risk of first and second marriage dissolution", Statistics Canada article (2006), No. 81, at pp. 23-6

Cummings, J.L., and Z.S. Khachaturian, *Definitions and diagnostic criteria, in clinical diagnosis and management of Alzheimer's disease*, S. Gauthier, ed. (London: Martin Dunitz Ltd., 1999)

Davidson, D., "Knowing One's Own Mind", *Proceedings and Addresses of the American Philosophical Association* (1987), 61, at pp. 441-54

Department of Justice Canada, Annotated Bibliography on Comparative and International Law Relating to Forced Marriage (August 2007), available online at: http://www.justice.gc.ca/eng/pi/fcy-fea/lib-bib/rep-rap/2007/mar/index.html#a01

Double, R., "Two Types of Autonomy Account" (1992), 22(1) Can. J. of Philosophy, at pp. 65-80

Dworkin, G., *The Theory and Practice of Autonomy* (New York: Cambridge University Press, 1988)

Elster, J., *Sour Grapes. Edition de la maison des sciences de l'homme* (Paris: Cambridge University Press, 1993)

Feinstein, A., *Clinimetrics* (New Haven: Yale University Press, 1987)

Frankfurt, H., *The Importance of What We Care About* (New York: Cambridge University Press, 1988)

Frankfurt, H., "Freedom of Will and the Concept of a Person" (1971), 68 J. of Philosophy, at pp. 5-20

Freeman, M.D.A., and C.M. Lyon, *Cohabitation without Marriage* (Aldershot, Hants.: Gower, 1983)

Friedmann, W.G., *Law in a Changing Society*, 2nd ed. (New York: Columbia University Press, 1972)

Glass, K., and M. Silberfeld, *Determination of Competence, in Clinical Diagnosis and Management of Alzheimer's Disease*, S. Gauthier, ed. (London, England: Martin Dunitz, 1996)

Goodman, D., B. Hall, P. Hewitt, H. Labes and H. Mason, *Probate Disputes and Remedies*, 2nd ed. (Bristol: Jordans, 2008)

Griffin, J., *Against the Taste Model, in Interpersonal Comparisons of Well-Being*, J. Elster and J.E. Roemer, eds. (New York: Cambridge University Press, 1991)

Groopman, J., *How Doctors Think* (Boston: Houghton Mifflin Co., 2007)

Halsbury, *Halsbury's Laws of England*, 4th ed. (London: Butterworths, 1974)

Harper, S., "Mature Societies: Planning For Our Future Selves" (2006), 135 Daedalus, vol. 1, at pp. 20-31

Haworth, L., *Autonomy: an essay in psychology and ethics* (New Haven: Yale University Press, 1986)

Hill, T.E.J., *Autonomy and Self-Respect* (New York: Cambridge University Press, 1991)

Hommel, P., L. Wang and J. Bergman, "Trends in Guardianship Reform: implications for the medical and legal professions" (1990), 18(3) Law, Med. and Healthcare, at pp. 213-26

Hurley, S.L, *Natural Reasons* (New York: Oxford University Press, 1989)

La Forest, A. Warner, *Anger & Honsberger Law of Real Property*, 3rd ed., looseleaf (Toronto: Canada Law Book, October, 2008)

Langbein, J.H., "The Twentieth Century Revolution in Family Wealth Transmission" (1988), 86 Mich. L. Review 722

Leslie, M.B., "The Myth of Testamentary Freedom" (1996), 38 Ariz. L. Rev. 235

Madigan, K., D. Checkland and M. Silberfeld, "Presumptions Respecting Mental Competence" (1994), 39(3) Can. J. of Psychiatry, pp. 147-52

Madigan, K., and M. Silberfeld, "Clinical Application of the Least Restrictive Alternative in Competency Assessments" (1993), 12 E.T.P.J., at pp. 282-92

Mill, J.S., *On Liberty*, H.B. Acton, ed. (London: J.M. Dent and Sons, 1972)

National Alliance for Caregiving & Zogby Int'l, Miles Away; The MetLife Study of Long-distance Caregiving 2 (2004), available online: www.caregiving.org/data/milesaway.pdf

Norton, E.C., and D.H. Taylor, "Equal Division of Estates and the Exchange Motive" (2005), 17 J. Aging & Soc. Pol'y 63

Oosterhoff, A.H.,"Consequences of a January/December Marriage: a Cautionary Tale" (1999), 18 E.T.P.J., 261-284

Payne, J.D., and M.A. Payne, *Canadian Family Law*, 3rd ed. (Toronto: Irwin Law, 2008)

Power, W. Kent, *Power on Divorce and Other Matrimonial Causes*, 3d ed. (Toronto: Carswell, 1976-1980)

Rand, D.C., "The Spectrum of Parental Alienation Syndrome" (1997), 15 Am. J. Forensic Psych. No. 3

Robertson, G.B., *Mental Disability and the Law in Canada*, 2nd ed. (Toronto: Carswell, 1994)

Rougeau, V.D., "No Bonds but those Freely Chosen: An Obituary for the Principle of Forced Heirship in American Law" (2008), 1 Civ. L. Comment, No. 3

Selkoe, D.J., "The Aging Mind: Deciphering Alzheimer's Disease and its Antecedents" (2006), 135 Daedalus, vol. 1, at pp. 58-67

Sharpe, G., "Guardianship: two models for reform" (1983), 4(1) Health Law in Canada, at pp. 13-23

Shaw Spaht, K., "Forced Heirship Changes: The Regrettable 'Revolution' Completed" (1996), 57 L.A. L. Rev. 55

Silberfeld, M., "New Directions in Assessing Mental Competence" (1992), 38 Canadian Family Physician, at pp. 2365-69

Silberfeld, M., "Social Competence in Cognitive Disorder", in *Prospects in Aging*, L. Abisch, ed. (Sandoz: Academic Press, 1993), at pp. 163-203

Silberfeld, M., "The Use of 'Risk' in Decision-Making" (1992), 11(2) Can. J. of Aging, at pp. 124-36

Silberfeld, M., "Hope, Loss and Entitlement: Lessons from the Oncology Situation" (1981), 26 Can. J. of Psychiatry, at pp. 415-18

Silberfeld, M., "The Psychology of Hope and the Modifications of Entitlement Near the End of Life", in *Attitudes of Entitlement: theoretical and clinical issues*, V. Volkan and T.C. Rogers, eds. (Charlottesville: University of Virginia Press, 1988)

Silberfeld, M., et al., "Choosing a Risky Treatment; Psychosocial Aspects of Risky Choice" (1988), 13(1) Psychiatry Journal, at pp. 9-11

M. Silberfeld, et al., "Legal Standards and the Threshold of Competence" (1993), 14(4) A.Q., at pp. 482-87

M. Silberfeld, et al., "Capacity Assessments for Requests to Restore Legal Competence" (1995), 10(4) Int'l J. of Geriatric Psychiatry, at pp. 191-97

Silberfeld, M., W. Corber and D. Checkland, "Acknowledgement of Limitations and Understanding of their Consequences in Mental Capacity Assessments" (1995), 13(3) Behaviourial Sciences and the Law, at pp. 381-90

Silberfeld, M., M. Finstad and B. Dickens, "Prescreening Competency Assessments" (1993), 26(3) Annals The Royal College of Physicians and Surgeons of Canada, at pp. 165-68.

Silberfeld, M., D. Stephens and K. O'Rourke, "Cognitive Deficit and Mental Capacity Evaluation" (1994), 13(4) Can. J. of Aging, at pp. 539-49

Statistics Canada,"Census snapshot of Canada-Population [age and sex]" (2006), available online at: http://www.statcan.gc.ca/pub/11-008-x/2007006/article/10379-eng.pTate, J.C., "Caregiving and the Case for Testamentary Freedom" (2008), 42 U.C. Davis L. Rev. 129

Treitel, G.H., *The Law of Contract*, 11th ed. (London: Sweet & Maxwell, 2003)

United Nations, Convention on Consent to Marriage, Minimum Age for Marriage and Registration of Marriages, Office of the High Commissioner for Human Rights. General Assembly Resolution 1763 A (XVII), November 7, 1962, entered into force 9 December, 1964

United Nations, *Towards a Society for All Ages*. International Year of Older Persons. (United Nations Department of Public Information, DPI/1964/G - September 1999)

United States Government, *President's Commission for the Study of Ethical Problems in Medicine and Biomedical and Behavioral Research: Making health care decisions* (Washington, D.C.: U.S. Government Printing Office, 1982)

Verma, S., and M. Silberfeld, "Approaches to Capacity and Competency: the Canadian view" (1997), 20(1) Int'l J. of Law and Psychiatry, at pp. 35-46.

Weisstub, D., *Enquiry on Mental Competency* (Queen's Printer of Ontario: Toronto, 1990)

Wilson, C., "The Century Ahead" (2006), 135 Daedalus, vol. 1, at pp. 5-8

Young, R., "Autonomy and the 'Inner Self'" (1980), 17 American Philosophical Quarterly 35-43

INDEX